FORGOTTEN COLORADO

NORTHERN REGION

Wishing you a lifetime
of adventures !! :-)

Heath Gay

HEATH A. GAY

AMERICA
THROUGH TIME®
ADDING COLOR TO AMERICAN HISTORY

AUTOGRAPHED
by the
author

America Through Time is an imprint of Fonthill Media LLC
www.through-time.com
office@through-time.com

Published by Arcadia Publishing by arrangement with Fonthill Media LLC
For all general information, please contact Arcadia Publishing:
Telephone: 843-853-2070
Fax: 843-853-0044
E-mail: sales@arcadiapublishing.com
For customer service and orders:
Toll-Free 1-888-313-2665

www.arcadiapublishing.com

First published 2022

Copyright © Heath A. Gay 2022

ISBN 978-1-63499-397-5

Typeset in Trade Gothic 10pt on 15pt
Printed and bound in England

CONTENTS

ACKNOWLEDGMENTS

Creating a book that requires extensive travel has its challenges during a global pandemic. Unlike the first two books in the *Forgotten Colorado* series, my interactions with others were very limited, and my ability to visit certain sites was directly impacted by federal, state, and local guidelines, which I was more than happy to abide by.

Despite being a lone ranger most of the time, some special folks came out to play and assist when Covid-19 restrictions were lifted. And for that, I want to thank Julissa Vega, Arlene Alvarez, and Alice Andrade-Cushman. All three of you should get an award for putting up with my non-stop history talk and never-ending "sudden" stops while driving. Your company meant so much. Thank you!

Growing up wasn't easy, by any stretch of the imagination. Having the two best sisters one could ever have sure helped get me to the place I'm at now. Heather and Heidi, this book is for you, with much love coming your way!

My sisters—Heidi and Heather.

ABOUT THE AUTHOR

HEATH GAY is a lifelong resident of Colorado with an extreme passion for experiencing and sharing all the Centennial State has to offer. For the last twenty years, he has been a nationally recognized fitness expert, assisting thousands of people with achieving their wellness dreams through organizations such as the National Personal Training Institute, Health Fitness, Ford Motor Credit, Noom, and Hiking University.

Currently based out of Colorado Springs, Heath is an avid hiker, having summited all fifty-four of Colorado's mountains over 14,000 feet. In his spare time, he explores Colorado, documenting historically significant, unique, abandoned, and must-see sites throughout the state.

You can learn more about Heath and all things Colorado at ColoradoFanClub.com.

The author, Arlene Alvarez, and Alice Andrade-Cushman at the entrance to Shipler's Silver Mine in Rocky Mountain National Park.

INTRODUCTION

An investment in knowledge pays the best interest.
Benjamin Franklin

From the rugged Rocky Mountains to the arid Pawnee National Grassland, Northern Colorado's varied landscapes have provided a playground and way of life for centuries. Originally, much of the region was a travel route and hunting ground for Native Americans, including the Ute, Arapahoe, and Apache tribes.[1] The early to mid-1800s saw an increased presence of traders and trappers, leading to several fort's being established. Four forts established during this time include Fort Vasquez, Fort St. Vrain, Fort Lupton, and Fort Jackson.[2] The 1860s through the 1890s brought two major milestones that expanded Northern Colorado into the agricultural and recreational powerhouse that it would become, and continues to be today. Those two events were the Homestead Act of 1862 and the railroad finding its way into the region.

The Homestead Act of 1862 was signed into law by Abraham Lincoln on May 20, 1862. The act allowed an individual to claim 160 acres of public land if three criteria were met. First, the person must live on the desired land for at least five years before filing for deed of title. Second, appreciable enough improvements must be made to the property. Third, a fee had to be paid to make the land ownership official. If one of those things was missing, the claim was denied.[3]

Now enter the railroad. The Denver Pacific Railway made its way into the Colorado Territory on September 15, 1869, with other railroad lines not far behind, opening up Northern Colorado lands and opportunities.[4] A faster, cheaper, more convenient mode of transportation, coupled with the Homestead Act of 1862 and high hopes, worked together to substantially grow Northern Colorado's population. Wildly enough, the Homestead Act of 1862 wasn't repealed until 1976 via the Federal Land Policy and Management Act of 1976.[3]

Today, Northern Colorado still holds tight to its transportation, agricultural, and exploration roots. The railroad continues to run through the region, being an important link for distribution of Colorado goods in the twenty-first Century. Thanks to the resiliency and ingenuity of ranchers and farmers with managing the dry land and unpredictable weather, Northern Colorado continues to thrive in regard to high quality produce and proteins. And for outdoor enthusiasts, Rocky Mountain National Park and the Pawnee National Grassland provide more than 715 square miles of adventure opportunities![5]

Forgotten Colorado: Northern Region focuses on historic, unique, abandoned, and must-see places throughout Northern Colorado. You will be exposed to twenty areas, and more than forty-five different sites that provide a glimpse into what life was like back in the day, and in some cases, how life continues today. By design, a lot has been left out of the book so that you can have your own unique experience when visiting each place. With that said, I want to touch on three important considerations we should ALL keep in mind when exploring Colorado:

1. BE A GOOD STEWARD.

Each of us is responsible for protecting Colorado's historic and natural resources, so that others can enjoy them in the future. Following the "Leave No Trace" ethics established by the Leave No Trace Center for Outdoor Ethics, is one way to be a good steward when exploring the state and locations profiled in this book:

Leave No Trace Principles:
1. Plan Ahead and Prepare
2. Travel on Durable Surfaces
3. Dispose of Waste Properly
4. Leave What You Find (Take only pictures.)
5. Minimize Campfire Impacts (Actually, don't EVER start a fire at these sites!)
6. Respect Wildlife (Including the local residents!)
7. Be Considerate of Other Visitors

2. KNOW YOU RIGHTS AS A PHOTOGRAPHER.

Knowing your rights as a photographer is important for ensuring a safe, enjoyable, and legal experience. Taking photographs and video of things that are plainly visible in public spaces is a constitutional right. Respect people's personal property and boundaries, and few issues should arise. With that said, there are some exceptions, such as taking pictures of people "inside" a house from a public spot or taking pictures of certain federal facilities. I am not a lawyer and this information does not constitute legal advice of any kind. Consult your individual state regulations and/or a lawyer for the most up-to-date laws governing photography and trespassing.

When in doubt as to the legality of your presence or picture taking, ALWAYS get the expressed verbal and/or written consent to enter a property or take pictures, BEFORE actually doing so. Whatever it is you are trying to photograph likely won't go anywhere soon, but you just might if you get busted for trespassing.

3. SPEND MONEY IN THE COMMUNITY.
It is important to support the communities we explore. They are providing an experience, and our visits have an impact on their resources. Have a meal, get gas and snacks, buy some souvenirs—it's the right thing to do. Plus, you might meet someone local that will share some stories!

Without further ado, let's get to it!

Forest Canyon Overlook in Rocky Mountain National Park. The path leads to an educational sign and a wooden bench that one could sit on to contemplate the information presented and amazing views.

GENERAL LOCATIONS FOR SITES IN THE BOOK

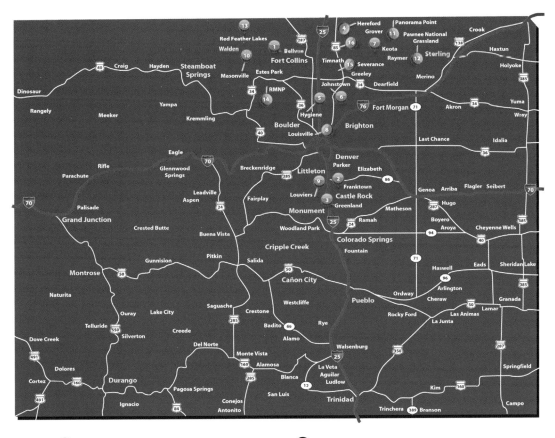

1 Bellvue

2 Franktown

3 Greenland

4 Hereford

5 Hygiene

6 Johnstown

7 Keota

8 Louisville

9 Louviers

10 Masonville

11 Colorado Tri-Points

12 Pawnee National Grassland

13 Red Feather Lakes

14 Rocky Mountain National Park (RMNP)

15 Severance

16 U.S. Highway 85 (Traveling North)
   - Platteville
   - Eaton
   - Ault
   - Pierce
   - Nunn

Map Credit: Derrick Cook

1

BELLVUE, COLORADO
A BEAUTIFUL VIEW

Jacob Flowers settled in Pleasant Valley, northwest of Fort Collins, back in 1873. Its location near prime agricultural land, railroads, and stone quarries made this area destined for growth and prosperity. Over time, Mr. Flowers established multiple businesses, including a mercantile, saloon, post office, horse racetrack, and others.[1] Though already known as Bellevue, the 28-acre townsite owned by Jacob Fowler would take until 1887 to be officially recorded and recognized. Not too long after, the second "e" in Bellevue was dropped in favor of the shortened name of Bellvue.[2]

In 1896, Bellvue was incorporated. This action was a testament to the strong economy and abundant opportunities available in the region at that time. Fast forward almost twenty years, and things have changed dramatically. With the stone quarries mined to exhaustion, and the railroads reducing service, many folks began moving away from Bellvue. The result was a dissolution of the town's incorporation status in 1914, and a heavier reliance on agriculture for survival.[3]

Uncle Jake's legacy is still strong today in Bellvue. Farming still reigns supreme, something he was heavily involved with and helped evolve while still alive. The original Flowers Store has been preserved and is still in use today as a community meeting center. Additionally, a post office still operates in Bellvue.

FASCINATING FACTS FROM THE PAST ABOUT BELLVUE

1900: The cause of a horrific outbreak of typhoid fever in Fort Collins was reported by the state epidemiologist to be caused by the careless actions of a nurse taking care of a typhoid patient in Bellvue. Rather than dispose of excrement and infected materials via burying the items, as instructed, she chose to the throw them into a nearby ditch. The result was contamination of the Poudre River and the water supply of Fort Collins.[4]

1903: The *Weekly Courier* stated that the population of Bellvue was 300 in 1903.[5] In contrast, as of 2019, Bellvue is estimated to have a population of around 1,500 residents.[6]

1915: An unknown person illegally shot and killed two cows and one deer in the hills near Bellvue. According to the newspaper article, "The law is very severe on the killing of deer and more so on the malicious killing of livestock. The penitentiary waits the man who did the killing."[7]

1918: The *Loveland Daily Herald* reported a massive rainstorm, stating that "The floods tore down thru the town of Bellvue taking out 300 feet of the railroad track and marooning a train. Water stood six feet deep around the old stone schoolhouse at Bellvue and washed away the west approach to the Poudre River bridge just east of Bellvue."[8]

1925: The Bellvue-Watson Fish Hatchery was built in 1924. Based on a 1925 column written in the *Estes Park Trail* newspaper, the hatchery had a capacity of ten million trout annually![9]

The front entrance to the Old Flowers Store and Bellvue Post Office, built in 1882. This building is the only commercial structure in Bellvue constructed out of locally quarried stone.

A side view of the Old Flowers Store and Bellvue Post Office. Since 1948, the building has been a community meeting center and home to Cache la Poudre Grange, Chapter 486.

The Bellvue Store as seen from the Old Flowers Store and Post Office.

The Bellvue Store building was built in 1900 and has served many roles since then. Most recently, it was a coffee shop and artist venue called Bellvue Bean.

A view of the Bellevue Store and Old Flowers Store through a large piece of art on the Bellvue Bean property.

The Bellvue Church of Christ was founded in 1911, with the church building constructed in 1912. This is the oldest Church of Christ congregation in Colorado that has remained at the same location.

Watson Lake at Watson Lake State Wildlife Area (SWA). A valid hunting or fishing license or SWA pass is required for everyone sixteen or older accessing any state wildlife area.

The Bellvue-Watson Fish Hatchery, located near the Cache la Poudre River, began operations in 1914. The Watson Lake Rearing Unit is responsible for raising hundreds of thousands of catchable trout that will be released in nearby bodies of water. This location is also home to the very important Colorado Parks and Wildlife's Fish Research Hatchery (FRH).

A look at part of the Noosa Yoghurt complex located at the historic Morning Fresh Dairy Farm (established in 1894). Tours are available to the public. Check out the Morning Fresh Dairy Farm website for more information (morningfreshdairy.com).

Above: Located on the Noosa Yoghurt property, Howling Cow Cafe offers baked goods, coffee drinks, Morning Fresh Dairy products, and a variety of Noosa yoghurt flavors.

Right: Did you know that "root beer float" milk is a real thing? For the adventurous, Howling Cow Cafe offers up several varieties of flavored milk to try out.

The Pleasant Valley School (left) was built in 1879 and is a rare example of a rural one-room schoolhouse. The wooden cabin to the right of the school is a superb example of how a cabin would typically be constructed during that timeframe (1870s-1880s).

The school foundation and walls were made from locally quarried sandstone. The original school bell was donated to the Bellvue Church of Christ and can be found on their church roof.

A very old one-room cabin sits next to the Pleasant Valley School.

2

FRANKTOWN, COLORADO
FRANK'S TOWN

Frank's Town was originally established in 1859 when Mr. James "Frank" Gardner settled in the area. Franktown's location along the popular Jimmy's Camp Trail made it a desirable place for travelers to visit, rest, and engage in commerce. In 1861, the settlement name was officially changed to Franktown, with the community becoming the Douglas County seat that same year (1861-1863).[1] Mr. Gardner was a busy man. During his time in the area, he was state senator, territorial legislator, representative, and postmaster of Franktown and Castle Rock, Colorado.[2]

Agricultural endeavors and ranching were important industries back in the day, and they continue to be so today. A visual and living symbol of Franktown's agricultural strength and community unity can be seen via the Pikes Peak Grange No. 163. This historic structure has been bringing people together and creating life-long memories since 1909.[1]

FASCINATING FACTS FROM THE PAST ABOUT FRANKTOWN

1913: Mr. Frank Wheeler passed away at the age of seventy-three. He was one of the oldest residents of Douglas County, which was established in 1861. Mr. Wheeler moved to Franktown back in 1875, after serving twice in the Civil War.[3]

1932: The Progressive Turkey Club of Franktown met at the Pikes Peak Grange No. 163 before leaving the building for a tour of local turkey farms, followed by lunch and guest speakers.[4]

1939: It was reported that all students attending the Franktown School had been exposed to polio, with two cases of infantile paralysis occurring and requiring medical attention. In lieu of shutting down, county officials determined that it would be best to forge ahead with school, keeping a watchful eye out for a major outbreak. To help prevent illness, each student had their throat and nose sprayed twice daily, and frequent temperature checks.[5]

1984: History was made when the Olympic Torch traveled through Franktown on its way to the opening ceremony for the 1984 Summer Olympics in Los Angeles.[6]

1987: The Franktown Post Office celebrated its 125th anniversary at the 13th Annual Franktown Festival. A special stamp was designed to commemorate the post office milestone, with a small quantity of those stamps available for purchase by festival attendees.[7]

Castlewood Canyon Dam was built in 1890 over Cherry Creek using locally quarried stone. Its overall construction was considered questionable for decades before it finally succumbed to a heavy summer of raining. The dam burst open around 1:00 a.m. on April 3, 1933, sending a 15-foot wall of water toward Denver. Massive destruction to homes and structures in the water's path, and two deaths, were the end result of the Castlewood Canyon Dam disaster.

Castlewood Canyon State Park contains a cornucopia of enjoyable outdoor opportunities via the ability to visit historic structures (dam and Lucas homestead), hike miles of superb trails, rock climb 300+ routes, or view well over 100 species of animals that include the Preble's meadow jumping mouse, golden eagle, Woodhouse's toad, fathead minnow, northern leopard frog, western territorial garter snakes, and massive turkey vultures.

The Franktown historical marker reads, "Franktown. Named for J. Frank Gardiner, a pioneer who settled here in 1859. First known as 'California Ranch,' it was a way station on the stage line between Denver and Sante Fe. In a stockade built here, neighbors found refuge from Indians in 1864. Franktown became the first county seat of Douglas County in 1861."

The Russellville Ranch property is the earliest settlement in Douglas County. Some of the more notable structures reportedly still on the property include the springhouse (1859), stage barn (1861), icehouse, and a dairy barn/ stable (1930).

The front entrance of the Pikes Peak Grange No. 163 building, built in 1909. Over 110 years later, and the historic structure is still being used for community gatherings and special events.

A back and side view of the structure. The Pikes Peak Grange No. 163 building was added to the National Register of Historic Places in 1990, due to its social and architectural significance.

Franktown Cemetery is one of the oldest, continually in-use cemeteries in Colorado, with its first burial occurring in 1870.

Left: The "Douglas County Historic Landmark" identifier is located near the front entrance of the cemetery. You will have to open and close a gate to get inside the cemetery.

Below left: Clara Kelly was the first person buried in the Franktown Cemetery. She passed away on June 21, 1870, at the age of twenty-one years, six months, and sixteen days old. The back of her headstone reads, "She was a kind and affectionate wife, a fond mother, and a friend to all."

Below right: James Frank Gardner was the inspiration behind the naming of Franktown. He lived from 1834 until 1904 and is buried near other Douglas County pioneers in the Franktown Cemetery.

3

GREENLAND, COLORADO
A LUSH VALLEY

In 1871, the Denver & Rio Grande Railroad found its way into the area. And like so many other Colorado communities that were born from the railroad, Greenland was established. Not long after, businesses and residents flocked to the region too. Quickly, Greenland became a vital shipping point for locally sourced lumber, milk, grain, cattle, and famous Colorado potatoes. In 1873, a post office was established that operated until 1959. According to an article in the *Tribune*, at one point "there were two blacksmith shops, a wagon-making shop, a saloon, a school that was used from 1892 to 1957, two stores and a hotel."[1]

The construction of a new Denver-Colorado Springs highway in the 1920s is credited with the start of Greenland's decline. As traffic and people were diverted away from the community, most businesses, and eventually the school, disappeared. Today, not much remains from those early glory days. The Greenland Ranch still raises animals and is the longest continuously operating cattle ranch in Colorado. Trains continue to roll through daily, carrying their cargo to other destinations. And for recreation, 3,600 acres can be accessed by hikers, bikers, and horseback riders via the Greenland Open Space trail system.[2]

FASCINATING FACTS FROM THE PAST ABOUT GREENLAND

1877: The *Colorado Springs Gazette* reported that B. W. Riggs was appointed to the position of postmaster for Greenland.[3]

1905: More than five years prior to 1905, Spencer Dicks was convicted of murdering O. R. Miner near Greenland, Colorado. Mr. Dicks discovered his girlfriend, Minnie Hutchinson, in what was described in this article as a "compromising position," with Mr. Miner. In return, Spencer shot Mr. Miner dead on the spot. Miss Hutchinson lied at Mr. Dicks' inquest, saying he had no reason to kill Mr. Miner, and then left the state before his trial. Mr. Dicks was left without a witness to his story and was subsequently convicted of murder. After years of built-up guilt, Miss Hutchinson returned to Colorado, set the record straight, and Mr. Dicks was released from the state penitentiary in 1905.[4]

1913: Mr. Alderman was delivering eighteen cans of milk to Greenland via wagon when his horses became spooked. The wagon overturned, causing Mr. Alderman, his two female companions, and the milk scheduled for delivery to be thrown to the ground. No major injuries were sustained, though only three cans of milk survived the incident.[5]

1952: A purebred Milking Shorthorn was sold by the Peters family of Greenland to Emil Rippe and Sons of Aurora, Colorado.[6] A Milking Shorthorn is one of the oldest breeds of dairy cattle. It was introduced into the United States in 1783.[7]

1980: The *Douglas County News-Press* disclosed that the historic Greenland Ranch was purchased for close to $11,000,000, by William Simon. Mr. Simon was the United States Secretary of the Treasury during the Nixon Administration. The Greenland Ranch property is said to be one of the largest single pieces of undeveloped land between Denver and Colorado Springs.[8]

The town of Greenland was created as a direct result of the Denver & Rio Grande Railroad arriving in the region back in 1871. Today, transport trains (no passenger) still operate in the area daily.

The Greenland Ranch was established in the 1870s and holds the distinction of being the oldest operating cattle ranch in Colorado. At its property peak, the Greenland Ranch spanned approximately 21,000+ acres, making it also one of the largest ranches in Colorado at that time. Thanks to conservation efforts, this area will remain one of the biggest tracts of undeveloped land between Denver and Colorado Spring for generations to come.

The iconic Red Barn of Greenland Ranch was built shortly after the original barn on property met its demise in 1922 by burning to the ground after a lightning strike. The massive Red Barn that replaced the original structure was said to be able to accommodate 100 head of callle, with additional room for wagons inside.

Above: Old structures that speak to Greenland's more bustling past.

Left: Just before entering the Greenland Open Space parking area, this intriguing wood structure can be found.

The northern entrance to the Greenland Open Space is down the road from the Greenland Ranch. Located near the parking lot is a structure that pays homage to a pioneering family of the region, the Higbys. The picnic pavilion is designed to reflect the original look of the Higby Mercantile, which operated in Greenland from 1907-1934.

Due to the preservation work of Douglas County and many others, this former parcel of the historic Greenland Ranch is available for public recreation. Greenland Open Space provides more than 3,000 acres and 11+ miles of superb trails that can be modified to accommodate beginner to advanced hikers and bikers. Horses are welcome, too!

Greenmont Cemetery was established in 1889 by the founder of Palmer Lake, Mr. W. Finley Thompson. Originally meant to be used as a "final resting site" for residents of Palmer Lake, Edward Thomas Kipps is the only person there with a formal headstone. Mr. Kipp emigrated from England to the United States at the age of twenty-seven, before dying in Palmer Lake one short year later in 1889 from tuberculosis.

Hidden in the trees and scrub oak just to the north of Edward Kipp's headstone is a memorial marker for the Dalton Family. The Dalton Family came to the Palmer Lake are in the 1880s, becoming valued members of the Palmer Lake region for generations to come.

The historic Charles Allis Ranch was established in 1911. The Allis family raised milk cows and prize-winning Hampshire sheep, along with seven kids!

4

HEREFORD, COLORADO
THE KING OF CATTLE

Originally called Devon, the town's location near the Colorado-Wyoming border and Pawnee National Grassland made it a prime spot for the railroad, ranching, and dry farming. Two of the biggest players in the cattle business in the late 1800s to early 1900s were Frank Benton's Ranch and the J. W. Iliff Land and Cattle Company. At some point prior to 1900, ranching became so dominant that the town name was changed from Devon to Hereford, in honor of the most prized breed of cattle raised in the region.[1]

Hereford would experience major challenges as a consequence of the Great Depression (1929-1939) and Dust Bowl (1930s) periods. Many businesses fizzled out, and the Hereford School closed in 1940. Though beaten and battered during those "dirty thirties," ranching and farming survived, and both continue in the region today.

FASCINATING FACTS FROM THE PAST ABOUT HEREFORD

1917: Seven escapees from a Colorado Springs jail were captured in Hereford.[2]

1919: As the eastern Weld County health officer, Dr. Olsen, was sent to Hereford to investigate reports of smallpox in the town. He found that almost everyone had been exposed to the disease and that smallpox had been present in the town for about a month.[3]

1923: For the low cost of $5.00, students at the University of Northern Colorado in Greely (then called the Colorado State Teachers College) could take a field trip to visit the unique geological formations at the Pawnee Buttes, with a stop at the Hereford Inn for a tasty dinner.[4]

1923: It was reported by *The Raymer Enterprise* that Dr. Martha K. J. Blanchard of New York would be opening a state-of-the-art cancer treatment hospital in Hereford later that year.[5]

1929: Robert Blake, of Hereford, was initiated into the Lambda Gamma Kappa Fraternity at the University of Northern Colorado (then called the Colorado State Teachers College).[6]

The idea to have a non-denominal church in Hereford was sparked in 1939 by three ladies known as the "Gospel Trio" (Gertrude Horn, Norma Erickson, and Helen Triboulet). In 1942, the former Coleman Church building was bought at an auction and relocated in 1943 to the foundation where it continues to sit today.

The church bell stands tall near the front entrance. On a different note, the first Easter sunrise service held at the Hereford Community Church was on April 24, 1946, a tradition that continues today.

The Home of Peace Cemetery was established in 1938, in a fairly desolate area about 10 miles from Hereford, and not too far from the Pawnee National Grassland.

It was reported in 1975 by the town clerk that the town records had been destroyed, and with that, the cemetery records. Therefore, very little is known about the cemetery, or the folks buried there prior to 1975.

The double sloped roof situation is a nice architectural touch for this large, old, and decaying structure. Bonus points for the abandoned truck camper in the yard!

A classic car, with classic whitewall tires, sits broken down next to what appears to be a vacant home in Hereford.

This garage is no longer in service—and hasn't been for decades.

Remnants of ranching at sunset.

An abandoned homestead sits silently decaying, showing a superb set-up for its time—a two-story house, several outbuildings, a well, windmill, and plenty of grazing space.

Another abandoned house in the Hereford region. A structural symbol reflecting a more prosperous time in the past.

5

HYGIENE, COLORADO
HEALTHIEST TOWN IN COLORADO

Reverend Jacob S. Flory came to the region in the 1870s as a representative of the German religious group known as the Church of the Brethren. During his eleven short years in Hygiene, Mr. Flory facilitated the opening of the first post office, helped build the impressive Church of the Brethren stone building, and opened the Hygiene House to treat folks suffering from tuberculosis.[1]

Hygiene is a pretty quiet place these days, just like it was back in the day. A few businesses are in operation, including the historic Mountain Fountain Store. Hygiene Hay Days in August of each year continues to be a celebrated event by many. Not to mention, the town's location just on the outskirts of busy Longmont, coupled with its beautiful scenery, make Hygiene a popular place for a long bike ride or a scenic drive.

FASCINATING FACTS FROM THE PAST ABOUT HYGIENE

1891: An advertisement in a newspaper for the Hygiene Jersey Dairy Farm claimed that "animals are all chosen from the best herds of Massachusetts. Not one of the lot is from a herd having a record of less than 300 pounds of butter per cow."[2]

1901: A Saturday night spelling competition was held at the Hygiene Grange. Jennie Heinley came out victorious as the spelling champion.[3]

1926: Ralph Blackburn died at the age of seventy-four in his Hygiene home, after a brief battle with an undisclosed illness. Before his death, Mr. Blackburn was one of the oldest prospectors living in Boulder County, having decades of mining experience.[4]

1926: J. B. Smith was hospitalized, suffering from what was called in the newspaper as a "general breakdown" due to his age. At eighty-nine years old, he was believed to be the oldest pioneer in Boulder County. It was reported that he was feeling better the following day.[5]

1926: The Council of Rural Women had an all-day meeting using the community room in the basement of the Hygiene School. Included on the agenda: attractive meal suggestions for the summer months, household conveniences costing less than one dollar, demonstration of an iceless refrigerator, presentation of a new egg beater in a brown bowl, and a round-table discussion on well planned picnic lunches.[6]

Two large trees guard the entrance to the Church of the Brethren, built by Reverend Jacob S. Flory in 1880, out of rough cut, natural stones quarried from Lyons, Colorado. The church cost approximately $2,000 to build.

A back view of the church, also called the Old Dunkard Church, showing a newer addition to the building. This structure is the last remaining Brethren church in Colorado. The building was added to the National Register of Historic Places in 1984, for its architectural and religious significance related to years 1875-1899.

The Hygiene Cemetery is located on the grounds of the Church of the Brethren, providing a resting place for folks since the late 1800s.

A row of headstones in the Hygiene Cemetery. Of note is a small cemetery across the street from the Church of the Brethren. Before Hygiene was called Hygiene, it was known as Pella. You can find the former Pella Cemetery just to the south of the church. It is now often referred to as Hygiene South Cemetery.

One of the most interesting headstones I have seen so far in a Colorado cemetery, a conglomeration of stones and shells!

The application for the first post office in Hygiene was applied for in 1883 by Reverend Jacob S. Flory. Residents continue to enjoy the benefits of local mail services, 139+ years later!

The Mountain Fountain is a popular place to visit in Hygiene, and one of the few places to stop in the immediate area for snacks, cold drinks, and unique healthy food fare. It is a very population destination for road cyclists, desiring a break during a long bike ride.

The Mountain Fountain Store is located in the former Clark's Food Store, built in 1945. This original sign from that time hangs on the ceiling in the current establishment.

The Country Convenience Store, located across the street from the Mountain Fountain Store, has been vacant for many years.

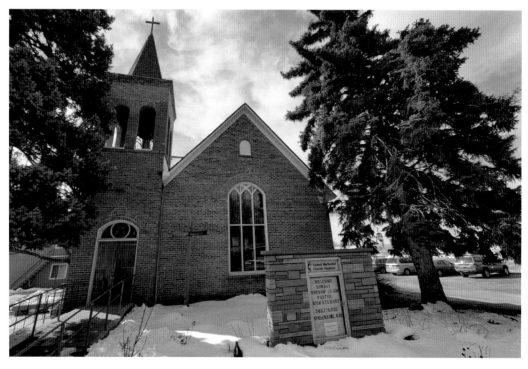

The Hygiene United Methodist Church was dedicated on January 21, 1906. The church and church body continue to be an integral part of the Hygiene community today.

6

JOHNSTOWN, COLORADO
LITTLE JOHN'S TOWN

With a new railroad being built through Loveland to reach the rich sugar beet farmland, Harvey J. Parish saw an opportunity to establish a new town along the route. Thus, in 1902, Mr. Parish secured a plat for Johnstown, with the community being named after his young son who, at the time, had been laid up in a hospital with an appendicitis. Johnstown would officially be incorporated in 1907. Along with excellent sugar beet crops and local sugar beet processing, Johnstown was also known for its high-quality dairy products.[1]

Some notable events related to Johnstown's history from the Johnstown Historical Society[2]:

1903: Post office officially opens
1903: First schoolhouse opens
1904: First National Bank of Johnstown opens
1904: New brick school built to accommodate larger student body
1911: Major fire destroys several businesses on Main Street
1923: Mr. Harvey J. Parish passed away
1924: The Johnstown Meteorite event occurred

FASCINATING FACTS FROM THE PAST ABOUT JOHNSTOWN

1905: In what was called a "disastrous storm," Johnstown residents endured a torrential rain and hail event that elevated the Little Thompson River to such a degree that it overflowed and caused the destruction of numerous buildings, bridges, and 100 feet of new railroad grade. No injuries were reported.[3]

1912: Johnstown celebrated the inaugural "Dairy Day," a festival set aside in honor of the "old faithful cow." More than 500 people attended the event, which included a cow contest, presentations by dairy industry experts, and milking machine demonstrations. In case you were wondering, first and second place winners for the best dairy cow were Holsteins.[4]

1914: In 1876, Colorado officially became a state, and Mr. T. A. Kirby was present when that historic day occurred. A Civil War veteran, he moved to Colorado in 1876 and homesteaded near Johnstown until his death in 1914 at age seventy-one.[5]

1915: The safe at the Johnstown Post Office was blown open. The burglars made away with a massive haul of $100 and a "large quantity" of stamps.[6]

1918: In an effort to counter the exorbitant costs and inefficiency related with transporting goods via railroad between Johnstown and Denver, W. T. Porter established the first auto truck transport service between the two towns. The Northern Colorado Automobile and Truck Company started with nine trucks, stopping at towns along the way between Denver and Johnstown, picking up and delivering freight as needed. To this day, Johnstown is a popular trucking town, having one of the most famous truck stops in the state![7]

Opening in 1952, Johnson's Corner has become a standard stop for truckers, travelers, and cinnamon roll connoisseurs. Since opening, Johnson's Corner has never closed, staying open 365 days a year to meet the never-ending needs of wandering souls.

The world-famous cinnamon rolls found at Johnson's Corner come in a wide variety of flavors depending on the season. Options can include cranberry, blueberry, caramel pecan, lemon, cinnamon raisin, chocolate cherry, key lime, and others.

The Johnson's Corner Chapel is a refuge for travelers and locals wishing to take a faith break. Located next to Johnson's Corner, services and community events are regularly offered at the chapel.

The cornerstone for the Masonic Temple in Johnstown was put in place on August 25, 1927, with the building being dedicated on March 27, 1928.

A neat mural on the side of the brick, State Farm Insurance building. A fire in the early 1900s destroyed several wooden structures on Main Street. This led to the use of bricks when rebuilding from the fire, and the use of bricks as a preferred material for future projects.

Built in 1916, this historic building is now the headquarters for radio station KHNC 1360 AM Radio, known as the "Roar of the Rockies" Conservative News Talk.

The view looking north from the intersection of N. Parish Avenue and Charlotte Street.

Harvey J. Parish, the founder of Johnstown, had this home constructed for his family in 1914. The design of the home is of particular historical significance, being the best local example of a Craftsman Bungalow style dwelling. The Town of Johnstown owns the home, with the Johnstown Historical Society responsible for the museum inside.

The United Methodist Church was the first church to be built in Johnstown (1904). In 1974, St. John the Baptist Catholic Church purchased the property, using the building until a recent move into an even bigger and more modern facility on the outskirts of town.

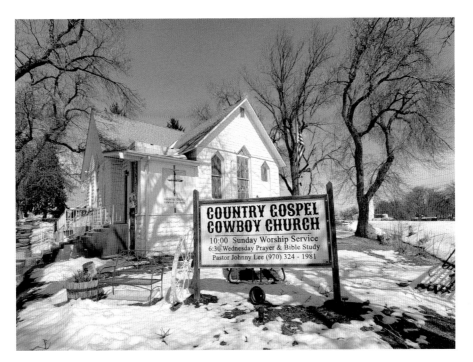

Country Gospel Cowboy Church began in 2013 with the intent of spreading God's word to cowboys and country folk. Based on the building materials and design, it most certainly is old and may have historical value, though I was unable to get more info on the structure.

In 1902, the United Brethren Church purchased 7 acres of land to be used as a cemetery. Originally called Elwell Cemetery, the name was later changed to Johnstown Cemetery in 1957, when the town officially took over responsibility for the managing the property.

Above left: This tree is hard to miss near the front of the Johnstown Cemetery. The face becomes more prominent the closer you get.

Above right: Lester March, from Post 70 of the American Legion, facilitated the placement of this memorial to veterans of all wars, back in 1933.

This particular headstone stood out from the others due to its design, size, and message.

7

KEOTA, COLORADO
DEATH FROM THE DUSTBOWL

The grasslands and prairies of Northern Colorado are as beautiful as they are remote. Nearly 100 years before this area became known as the Pawnee National Grassland (PNG), it was a destination for would-be farmers, ranchers, and railroad folks looking to take advantage of the Homestead Act of 1862.

One of the most significant towns in the PNG was Keota, Colorado. Keota was originally settled in the early 1880s by two sisters, Mary and Eva Beardsley. In 1888, Keota was sold to the Lincoln Land and Cattle Co. to be used as a railroad station stop.[1] With the railroad now traveling through the previously isolated area, numerous settlements and small towns sprang up through the region. Before long, over a thousand people were spread out across the grassland. The primary draws to the area were farming, ranching, and railroad work. Despite the influx of people, and settlements being established, Keota remained the most vital town and community resource in the region until the 1940s.

The early days of Keota (1890s-1920s) were full of challenges. Yet, it was a time of happiness and prosperity that would last for several decades, until a drought came in the 1920s. Dry land made it very tough to farm, making crop stability challenging and not very profitable. New dry farming techniques were becoming available and utilized, but it was too late. The Dust Bowl in the "Dirty Thirties" was the final nail in the region's farming coffin. The unrelenting wind wreaked havoc on the topsoil, making the land unfarmable. Most folks abandoned the grassland or sold their land to the government via a buyback program to assist devastated Dust Bowl regions. The Pawnee National Grassland of Colorado was established in 1960, using land purchased during the Dust Bowl land buyback period. We now have 193,000 acres of recreational possibilities available due to the unfortunate circumstances that occurred back in the 1930s.[2]

One man that lived through the boom and bust of Keota is Clyde Stanley. In fact, to many, Keota and Clyde Stanley are synonymous. He was the glue that held Keota, and the grassland region, together—especially since he produced the local newspaper and owned a general store for decades. Much of what we know historically about Keota and the surrounding areas comes from photographs and written documents that Clyde produced.

Arriving in Keota in 1910, Clyde established a homestead and began to publish the *Keota News* newspaper. As time passed, he would own a garage, general store, start several other publications, and serve as land commissioner, and eventually Clyde became the entire town government as the population dwindled.[3]

Notably, in the early 1970s, Pulitzer Prize winning author James Michener stayed in Keota and consulted with Clyde Stanley while writing the landmark book on Colorado titled *Centennial*. Clyde Stanley is mentioned in the book's dedication, a testament to his contribution to the book and friendship with James Michener.[3]

FASCINATING FACTS FROM THE PAST ABOUT KEOTA

1911: *The Idaho Springs Sifting-News* reported that, "This locality has begun negotiations to secure a government experiment station. The idea is to try various methods of planting, cultivating and other farm work and also to experiment in growing grains and grasses suitable for eastern Weld County."[4]

1918: Fourteen members of the Domestic Science Club were treated to the skillful instruction of Miss Mildred Krum, as she demonstrated how to make jello (general term for gelatin containing desserts) with whipped cream and fruit cake.[5]

1913: The Keota School Board voted to initiate a nine-month school term, moving away from the financially forced seven-month program previously implemented. It was determined that students in the Keota system deserved the same opportunities that other, longer established districts enjoy, thus the change was made to ensure Keota students did not fall behind.[6]

1922: Keota held its first annual Community Fair to much fanfare. One example of the event being a success can be seen in the fact that there were 200+ entrants alone in the sewing and fancy work category.[7]

1923: Returning home from a basketball game in Keota, seventeen-year-old Melvin Wertz complained of being "pushed off his feet" during the excitement of the game, and wrist pain. Once home, his mother bandaged the wrist and Melvin went to bed. Shortly after going to bed, he complained of difficulty breathing and passed away before help could arrive.[8]

A view of the most prominent structures remaining in Keota, from left to right: water tower, Keota Methodist Church (background), Clyde Stanley's home, Clyde Stanley's general store, and Auriel Sandstead's yellow house.

Clyde Stanley's two-story home not only has a unique design, but it's also conveniently located right next to where he spent most of his time.

This building once housed Clyde Stanley's general store, printing presses, and the Keota Post Office. Mr. Stanley brought the first newspaper to Keota in 1911, with a continuous run until 1923.

The "Yellow House" belonged to Auriel Sandstead, Clyde Stanley's niece. Known for her quilting passion and skills, she would regularly hold quilting get-togethers in the home, drawing folks from all over the state and country. Mrs. Sanstead was inducted into the Colorado Quilting Council Hall of Fame.

A view of what remains inside the red brick building that Clyde Stanley used for his various businesses over the years.

Scattered around the Keota townsite, many old foundations and relics from the past can be found.

The Keota Methodist Church was built in 1918. Over time, the church has lost its distinctive bell tower and front entrance stairs.

Looking at the backside of the structures located on Roanoke Avenue, as seen from the Keota Methodist Church.

The front entrance to the Keota Cemetery, which was established in 1911.

Clyde Stanley lived in Keota for sixty-three years. He passed away on January 8, 1976, at the age of eighty-eight.

A barren and wind-swept landscape contains the remains of those that found this place to be their home, and where the heart is.

Auriel Josephine Oram Sanstead lived from 1923-2007. The back of her headstone reads, "NorthP, East, South, and West, The Directions From Which Keota Winds Blow The Best. Thus The Winds Of Change Bring Starts And Stops And Begin Again! Cest la vie!"

8

LOUISVILLE, COLORADO
THE NORTHERN COALFIELD

I f one word had to be chosen to describe Louisville, that one word would be "coal." The first coal mine in the area was established in 1877 (Welch Mine), with Louis Nawatny platting the town of Louisville in 1878. One of the things that made Louisville incredibly unique compared to most coal towns in Colorado is that the coal miners worked where they lived. The coal mines were either in town or very close to it. In fact, the Acme Mine, located in the center of town, produced nearly 2,000,000 tons of coal! Relatively safe work conditions and decent wages for the day attracted a robust workforce and population. All totaled, thirty mines operated in or around Louisville.[1]

Despite favorable work conditions and wages, Louisville was not without problems. Labor disputes in the Northern Coalfield where Louisville was located impacted the town for several years (1910-1914), including acts of violence. It has been reported that the northernmost skirmish of the Northern Coalfield War occurred in Louisville.[2]

Unfortunately, the coal in the Louisville region was of inferior quality, making it more expensive and dangerous to transport. The sub-bituminous coal had the possibility of self-combustion if moved too great a distance. Coal quality, cost to procure, and low demand all contributed to the final Louisville coal mine closing up shop in 1952.[2]

Today, Louisville is a bustling city, with an estimated 20,000+ residents. The rich history, beauty, relative solitude, and close proximity to much larger towns such as Boulder, Broomfield, and Longmont make it an ideal place to live. In fact, Louisville has been named by multiple notable magazines and organizations throughout the 2000s as one of the top places to live and raise a family (*CNN, Money,* and *Family Circle*).[2]

FASCINATING FACTS FROM THE PAST ABOUT LOUISVILLE

1901: Two hundred Colorado Knights Templar attended the *Grand Encampment* in Louisville that year.[3]

1901: After almost nine months on strike, coal miners from the Northern Coal and Coke Company, with mines located in Eerie, Lafayette, and Louisville, began mining again for the first time in the twentieth century.[4]

1905: *The Eerie News* reported that the "Louisville stork called at the home of Mr. and Mrs. John Williams Saturday and left a big boy. The mother and son are doing nicely."[5]

1906: The Woodmen of the World held a special picnic in Eldorado Springs for surrounding communities, with a special train picking up residents in Louisville to transport them to and from the event. The Louisville Band provided the music.[6]

1977: "Operation I.D." began as a city-wide initiative to curb burglaries in town. Implemented and monitored by the Louisville Police Department, participants were instructed to mark their possessions using a "special engraving marker" provided by the police. Belongings needed to have the owner's social security number (SS#), along with the letters "CO" marked on each item. Serial numbers were then provided to the police department for easier tracking, in case of a theft.[7] Can you imagine having your SS# on all your valuables nowadays?

The Louisville Historical Museum is housed within the former Jacoe Grocery & Market building. Built in 1903, the store provided goods to the community until closing in 1958. The structure lay dormant until the 1980s, when the City of Louisville procured the property.

The Jordinelli House was moved to the Louisville Historical Museum property in 2001, from its original location at 1100 La Farge Avenue. The Queen Ann style home was built in 1904 by Frank and Rose Jordinelli.

Originally built and used as an overflow school for first and second graders (1894-1920), this historic red brick building also once housed the Chinook Library, a recreation center for the Lions Club, a senior center, and currently, the Louisville Center for the Arts.

Due to the availability of good coal mining jobs, many Italian families found their way to Louisville, becoming forever tied to the success, culture, and history of the region. Not only did Louisville have an area east of the railroad tracks known as "Little Italy," the homes on La Farge Avenue were primarily built and owned by Italians. This house is a classic example of a home that can be found on La Farge Avenue.

The Louisville United Methodist Church was built in 1892 and holds the distinction of being the oldest church in Louisville still worshipping in their original building. Until the 1970s the round window at the front of the church was covered, because sun glare bothered the various ministers' eyes.

Anthony C. V. Romeo built this exquisite home in 1907. It is Louisville's only historic home made from stone. Built out of rock obtained from Marshall, Colorado, it was eventually traded in 1919 by Mr. Romeo for a Denver pool hall.

The Louisville Arboretum is a tree lover's dream, showcasing more than seventy-five different tree species. Visitors can enjoy a leisurely walk along one of the designated paths, have a picnic at the pavilion, or get fit using the workout circuit.

One of the more unique features of the Louisville Arboretum would be the exercise stations that are spread out amongst the trees and along the pathways. What a wonderful place to work the mind, and the body. Learn and burn!

The Louisville Law Enforcement Memorial at Helburg Park was established in 2015 to honor all law enforcement officials and emergency responders in the area. The project was inspired by the tragic murder of Officer Victor Helburg on October 28, 1915, by a fruit vendor unwilling to pay for his fruit vending license. Mr. Helburg, as of the printing of this book, is the only Louisville police office to be killed in the line of duty.

The Casa Alegre Mexican Restaurant & Cantina is located in the historic Lackner Building. Joseph Lackner, a successful Louisville business owner, hired Herman H. Fischer to build the structure in 1904. During it's time, the Louisville Grocery, Track Inn, Pine Street Junction, and now Casa Alegre, have all called the Lackner Building home.

Harper Lake in Louisville is also home to the Leon A. Wurl Wildlife Sanctuary, a beautiful place to take a walk, look for animals, or have a picnic.

The Harper Lake Model Yacht Club builds and races remote controlled yachts at the lake. Racing season usually runs from April to November, with club members typically meeting on Saturdays to race at Harper Lake.

Above left: The Louisville Cemetery was established in 1892, thanks to the coordinated efforts of the Independent Order of Odd Fellows, Knights of Pythias, and Improved Order of Red Men. The World War Honor Roll marker was erected in 1924 by the residents of Louisville and vicinity under the auspices of The Women's Club.

Above right: George and Laura Ellis took care of the Louisville Cemetery from the 1930s until the 1970s. During that time, they made many favorable changes to the property. One notable improvement is a storage shed made from local rocks (Eldorado Springs), with a reinforced roof made from rails taken from a local coal mine.

9

LOUVIERS VILLAGE, COLORADO
THIS TOWN IS DYNAMITE!

Louviers Village was established during the years of 1906-1908, solely to house staff and family associated with the Du Pont Dynamite Factory, located just on the outskirts of town. Originally called Toluca until 1907, the area was ideal for explosives production due to its close proximity to railroad lines, abundant pool of potential workers (Denver), and location to the vast number of mines purchasing dynamite. At its peak, the company town had close to 100 homes, a post office, school, church, community parks, hotel, ballfield, and the extremely popular Louviers Village Club.[1]

Dynamite was a booming business back in the early 1900s. According to the *Colorado Encyclopedia*, "in its first year, the plant produced an average of 585,000 pounds of dynamite per month. At its height in the 1950s, it churned out more than two million pounds per month. It usually operated around the clock, three shifts per day, though it closed on weekends."[1] A few of the more notable Colorado locations that used Du Pont dynamite from the Louviers plant include Climax, the Pikes Peak Highway, and the Eisenhower-Johnson Tunnel.[1] By the time the Du Pont Dynamite Factory shut down operations in 1971, it had produced more than 1 billion pounds of dynamite.[2]

In 1962, Du Pont decided to sell Louviers Village, slow down dynamite production at the factory, and shortly thereafter, completely leave the area. Newer forms of explosives (less volatile), increased costs, and a lower demand for dynamite all contributed to the decision to shut down operations. Employees were given first dibs to purchase homes in Louviers Village, with Du Pont later donating the community parks and close to 900 acres to Douglas County.

Today, Louviers continues to be a quiet community, with fewer than 300 residents.[3] Many of the original homes have been restored, maintaining the look and feel of the company town. In 1999, Louviers Village was added to the National Register of Historic Places due to its industrial, social planning, and community significance.[4]

Fascinating Facts From the Past About Louviers

1958: An article written in honor of the 50th Anniversary of the Du Pont Company's Louviers Explosives Plant opening (1908) mentioned that more than 700,000,000 pounds of explosives had been produced up to that point.[5]

1965: Nancy Moore, a resident of Louviers as a child while her father worked for the Du Pont Company, came in ninth place on September 11, 1965, at the Miss America Pageant. She also won the Top Talent award for her captivating piano solo.[6]

1971: *The Douglas County News* reported that the Du Pont Explosives Plant in Louviers would be closing that summer. Decreased demand for dynamite, coupled with other cost-effective explosives options on the market, contributed heavily to the decision.[7]

1974: Fourteen out of fifteen tree samples taken from Louviers for Colorado State University's June report came up positive for Dutch Elm Disease (DED). DED is a fungal infection that attacks the circulatory system of the tree, causing a slow discoloration and death over time.[8]

1974: A Cessna 182 crashed near Louviers, with five passengers onboard. Despite the destructive nature of the crash, everyone survived.[9]

The Louviers Village sign and historical marker can be found at the south end of town on Louviers Boulevard, across the street from the Faith Evangelical Free Church.

The Louviers Community Presbyterian Church was built in 1927. Of note is the fact that this was the only building not directly built by Du Pont, and it remained the only church in Louviers while still a company owned town (pre-1962).

It was important to build a sense of community in a company owned town. The Louviers Village Club was built in 1917 to be a place that would bring people together and provide value to the community, which it did and continues to do so today via public and private events. For the bowling fans out there, the Louviers Village Club contains the oldest continuously used bowling alley in Colorado. Get your "Turkey" on!

Above left: A small pull-off at the intersection of Main Street and Louviers Drive will get you to a parking spot right by a Douglas County trail. Taking the paved trail (north) will lead to remnants of a railroad line that served the Du Pont Factory, as well as the original sign and former entrance to the factory itself. It has been a long time since a train transporting explosives has served the Du Pont Dynamite Factory.

Above right: The original Du Pont Dynamite Factory sign (*circa* 1908) is virtually unreadable. It is tucked away in the trees and greenery, just off the paved trail and to the left (when looking at the gate).

The former Du Pont Dynamite Factory entrance. Another company now occupies the property.

10

MASONVILLE, COLORADO
HOME OF THE 3RD *EPANTERIAS* EVER DISCOVERED

James Robinson Mason came to the Buckhorn Valley in 1885, and quickly became a successful rancher and farmer. He was the first person to bring the Red Poll breed of cattle into Colorado, delivered the first carload of potatoes ever to be sent down from the Buckhorn, and was a grower of the coveted Dutchess of Oldenberg apple. With the discovery of gold in the Buckhorn Valley, Mr. Mason established Masonville in 1896.[1]

A hotel, general store, and several other buildings were built in Masonville in preparation for the anticipated gold prospector population explosion. Unfortunately, the gold ore ended up being not just low in quality, but even lower in quantity. The expected gold boom quickly turned out to be a bust. In lieu of gold, stone quarries in the region provided another mining opportunity.[2]

Of particular note is the discovery of the "Masonville Monster" in a stone quarry near Masonville. The *Los Angeles Times* described the dinosaur as "one of the most ferocious dinosaurs that ever roamed the Earth—a giant, ugly beast with a jaw so big and powerful it could devour a 1,400-pound fellow dinosaur in a single gulp. It would have eaten about 40 tons of meat every year and was equipped with claws that seem to be the longest and strongest of any meat-eating dinosaur that ever lived."[3]

FASCINATING FACTS FROM THE PAST ABOUT MASONVILLE

1912: Kenneth K. Kane was serious when he told his wife that he only wanted to spend Christmas with her, and her alone. So, when she traveled to her hometown of Masonville to get her parents so as to bring them back to their Denver house for the holiday, Mr. Kane committed suicide.[4]

1915: The widow of John Mason (founder of Masonville), surprised everyone by marrying longtime bachelor, and ranching neighbor, Samuel Steele. A handful of friends and the bride's seven children were present for the Denver wedding.[5]

1917: Wallace Williams was reported to be the first "slacker" taken into custody from Larimer County, and Colorado in general. According to Wikipedia, during World War One, "the word "slacker" was commonly used to describe someone who was not participating in the war effort, specifically someone who avoided military service, equivalent to the later term draft dodger."[6] Mr. Williams refused to register for military service and was subsequently arrested. It was later determined that Mr. Williams was "mentally deficient" for service by the attending camp physician, and he was released back to his home in Masonville.[7]

1922: The Board of Education of the Masonville School determined it was in the best interest of the students (about thirty) to bring in a doctor to have them vaccinated against smallpox. The county physician and health officer, Dr. T. C. Taylor, was called in to make the shots happen.[8]

1927: Roy Hyatt tracked and killed a large mountain lion near his Masonville ranch. The animal was reported to be seven feet in length and around 140 pounds. The District Attorney for Loveland, Mr. Romans, purchased the skin for $25.[9]

Travelers to Masonville will see this sign on Buckhorn Road, just past the Masonville Mercantile building.

The Masonville Mercantile was built in the late 1890s. It changed ownership a couple of times before being moved in 1921 from its original location, to where it sits now.

An interesting old building can be found just across the road from the Masonville Mercantile.

Several additions have been added to the Masonville Mercantile over the years, but the store continues to maintain its old-time feel. There is a wide variety of vintage clothing, tons of antiques, unique gifts, and plenty of drinks and snacks to get you to your next location.

The jail cell in the picture came from the Loveland Jailhouse. It was purchased at an auction and added to the Masonville Mercantile property in the 1990s.

The jail cell taken from the Loveland Jailhouse was used from 1909-1966. The accommodations do not look comfortable or very welcoming.

There is so much to see at the replica wild west town across the street from the Masonville Mercantile.

For the antique farm equipment aficionado, the variety of old machines will bring a smile to the face.

Boot Hill is a mock wild west cemetery with humorous headstones. I won't spoil them for you but will share one epitaph. "J. Yeast (1912) He Will Rise No More."

The "Little Stone Church on the Hill" was dedicated on November 19, 1911. The building was built from locally sourced lumber and stone. The church has undergone expansion and modernization over the years and continues to serve the community today.

The Rhodes Family Cemetery is located on the Buckhorn Presbyterian Church property. The marker on the stone wall reads: "This Memorial Fence Erected By Friends of the Rhodes Family. 1966."

11

PAWNEE NATIONAL GRASSLAND, COLORADO
SHORTGRASS SERENITY

The Pawnee National Grassland (PNG) is a natural and geological wonder located in Northern Colorado. Stretching over 193,000 acres (315 square miles), the PNG is a part of the shortgrass plains of North America and consists of an astounding eleven different vegetation zones. The animals are plentiful in the region and include the lark bunting (Colorado state bird), mountain plover, burrowing owl, golden eagle, prairie falcons, bison, deer, rabbits, rodents, and much more.[1,2]

The PNG would experience a time of popularity from the 1890s until the 1930s, thanks to the Homestead Act and high hopes that dry farming techniques would succeed. Unfortunately, the Great Depression and the Great Dust Bowl were a double whammy on the region, creating a mass exodus of residents forced to seek livelihoods elsewhere.[1]

Today, the PNG continues to be sparsely populated, with the natural gas industry heavily active in the area. Recreational opportunities abound, including camping, picnicking, horseback riding, and star gazing. The Pawnee Buttes are the dominant feature drawing hikers and explorers to the area. For the serious bird watcher, the PNG is an internationally known birding area, complete with a 21-mile automobile birding tour. History aficionados will enjoy driving the remote dirt roads of the PNG looking for remnants of the past, including old homesteads, abandoned structures, and pioneer cemeteries.[2]

Fascinating Facts From the Past About the Pawnee Buttes (within the PNG)

1904: An article in the *Clear Creek Democrat* stated that "hundreds of bald-headed Rocky Mountain eagles build their nests and rear their young on the buttes, which are more than 200 feet high." Additionally, the article mentioned a Sterling, Colorado, fire company using ladders to scale one of the buttes, with the men planting the stars and stripes on the top.

1917: In an unfortunate event that even the victim would mention regretting before she died, Mrs. Charles Bigelow, eighteen years old and living near the Pawnee Buttes, ingested a fatal amount of strychnine after a short dispute with her husband about ranch and housework. Though she lived for several hours after the self-inflicted poisoning, there was nothing that could be done, and she passed away later that night.[4]

1925: Quoting the *Raymer Enterprise*: "Reminder of the millions of years so far back in the past that Rameses was a miser and Jezebel was a twentieth century flapper, abound at Pawnee Buttes several miles north of New Raymer where skeletal remains of extinct prehistoric monsters, such as the odd giraffes, camels, saber-tooth tigers, dinosaurs, are easily found."[5]

1925: Police found an elaborate and illegal distillery in a large cave (18 ft. x 25 ft.) near the Pawnee Buttes. The bootleg operation included two copper boilers and one forty-gallon still, with a daily output maximum of around fifty-gallons. Each gallon sold for approximately $20, making this a very lucrative business. One-hundred and four gallons of the finished product were confiscated by the authorities, with most being destroyed by fire.[6]

1954: The *Gazette Telegraph* reported in 1954 that "the Pawnee Buttes is the world's most famous cemetery of extinct animals, the ancestors of today's camel and horse."[7]

Bring binoculars, patience, and plenty of snacks, as you take on the PNG birding tour in your vehicle. The 21-mile, self-guided excursion, will put you in position to view and experience 300+ confirmed species that are known to be in the area.

The Pawnee Buttes Trail is approximately 1.5 miles long. The west butte is within the PNG, with the east butte on private property. Both are approximately 300 feet tall. Two interesting facts about the Pawnee National Grassland: 1. Deep underground, there multiple Minuteman missile silos protecting the nation. 2. North America's largest aquifer is ironically underneath the extremely dry PNG (Ogalalla Aquifer).

12

RED FEATHER LAKES, COLORADO
COLORADO'S FINEST PLAYGROUND

John Hardin settled in the Red Feather Lakes region in 1871. Primarily known for ranching and timber mills prior to the early 1900s, things would take a major shift in the 1920s with the formation of the Redfeather Mountain Lakes Association.[1] The Association sought to make the area a recreational haven complete with multiple lakes, 100+ cabins, a golf course, tennis courts, rodeo grounds, ranch school, and a rifle range. Though many of the amenities never manifested, it is interesting to note that a silver fox farm for making fur coats was established and operated into the 1950s.[2]

Red Feather Lakes never did see the population surge that was expected and hoped for by investors, despite it being touted in brochures as "Colorado's Finest Playground."[1] The Great Depression and World Warr II did not help the situation either, as attention and resources were diverted toward other things besides recreational pursuits. Today, Red Feather Lakes is still a quant village, with an emphasis on recreation and an eye on preserving its rich history. The Red Feather Historical Society has done a superb job preserving, protecting, and making available online resources and in-person access to historical artifacts and sites, such as the Robinson Cabin. While you're in the neighborhood, keep an eye out for Gnome Road with hidden gnomes and elves dotting the roadside and tree-lined landscape. The Great Stupa of Dharmakaya is also a sight to behold and worth a visit when near Red Feather Lakes.

FASCINATING FACTS FROM THE PAST ABOUT RED FEATHER LAKES

1936: Seniors from Colorado State University (CSU) went to Red Feather Lakes for their annual "Sneak Day." Hiking, horse-back riding, card playing, and dancing were on the docket for the day. One-hundred students participated in this school supported event.[3]

1939: Red Feather Lakes Postmaster Goldie Hastings had the distinctive honor of heading the reception committee at the 39th annual convention of the National Association of Postmasters, which included teatime at the White House with Mrs. Franklin D. Roosevelt.[4]

1942: The State Game and Fish Department (SGFD) attempted to buy the entire Red Feather Lakes chain for $22,500. The intent was to create an impressive recreational site, fishing resort, and updated fish hatchery. It was determined by Colorado Governor Carr that based on the original terms of the contract, the SGFD could not purchase the lakes. Thus, the deal fell through.[5]

1948: Three lakes within the Red Feather Lakes chain were poisoned with derris root powder by the State Game and Fish Department in an effort to kill all fish within, thereby eliminating undesirable species (Dowdy, Twin, and Bellaire Lakes). Once the water was safe, the lakes were restocked with rainbow trout and closed to fishing until the fish were of legal size.[6]

1982: *The Louisville Times* reported that the cost to cut down a Christmas tree in the Red Feather Lakes area was $5 that year.[7] The cost to obtain a permit to cut down a Christmas tree in the same area in 2020 was $20.[8]

Dayton Robinson and his family came to Red Feather Lakes (RFL) from New York, building this cabin in 1889. Originally located on private property, the Rocky Mountain Dharma Center donated the cabin to the RFL Historical Society. In 1995, the Robinson Cabin was moved to its current location, with a 1996 opening to the public as the RFL Cabin Museum. The key to do a self-guided tour can be obtained from the RFL Community Library.

This stack stood out, in contrast to a somewhat barren piece of land. Its history? A mystery.

13

ROCKY MOUNTAIN NATIONAL PARK, COLORADO
MONTAIGNES DE ROCHE

Long before Rocky Mountain Nation Park (RMNP) became established, the area was inhabited and visited by Paleoindian hunters, Archaic hunter-gatherers, Native Americans, Spanish explorers, French fur traders, cattle ranchers, miners, and early tourists looking to explore the outdoors.[1] Today, the area is a historical and recreational dream come true, with more than a dozen sites within the park listed on the National Register of Historic Places, over 350 miles of trails to play on, abundant wildlife, and views that will take one's breathe away![2]

A very small sampling of important dates related to RMNP from the National Park Service website[1]:

10,000 BC: Clovis Paleoindian hunters enter the park as the glaciers retreat.

1200-1300 AD: Ute enter North Park and Middle Park and RMNP.

1500: Apache are in the high country, including the park.

1800s: Arapaho make first appearance in the park.

1820: Stephen A. Long's expedition views Longs Peak while searching for the source to the Platte River.

1858: Joel Estes enters what is now Estes Park and starts a ranch.

1868: John Wesley Powell, William Byers, and others make the first ascent of Longs Peak (14,259 feet).

1915: Rocky Mountain National Park officially established on January 26, 1915.

1929-1933: Trail Ridge Road constructed. With a length of 48 miles, cresting higher than 12,000 feet, Trail Ridge Road is the highest paved "through road" in the United States.

FASCINATING FACTS ABOUT RMNP[3]

1. The area that makes up RMNP was originally acquired through the Louisiana Purchase in 1803. As of 2019, RMNP is one of the top five most visited National Parks in the country with around 4.6 million visitors each year.
2. RMNP is more than 265,000 acres, with impressive elevation variations that go from about 7,600 feet, all the way up to 14,269 feet (Long's Peak).
3. There have been more than 1,000 varieties of wildflowers identified in RMNP, 280+ species of birds are known to live in the park, and about 400 bighorn sheep call RMNP home.
4. According to the U.S. Department of the Interior, the National Park Service is in possession of 33,465 cultural objects, 294 works of art, 10,495 biological specimens and 455 geological specimens that are all related to the RMNP area. Some of the items can be seen by checking out the various visitor centers and other public places in the park.

The Beaver Meadows Visitor Center (formerly named the Rocky Mountain National Park Administration Building) was completed in 1967 and is the busiest visitor center in RMNP. Designed by a protégé of famous architect Frank Lloyd Wright, the structure was specifically designed to blend into its environment, which it does pretty well! The visitor center became a National Historic Landmark in 2001, due to its architectural significance and relationship with Mission 66.

The Moraine Park Visitor Center building was constructed in 1923 and originally served as a recreational center for the Moraine Lodge. It is the only remaining structure associated with the resorts in the Moraine Park area. The structure was added to the National Register of Historic Places in 1976 due to its social and recreational significance. Currently, along with being a visitor center, the building houses an interactive museum for RMNP guests, with an outdoor amphitheater close by.

Above left: William Allen White (1868-1944) was a newspaper editor, Pulitzer Prize winning journalist, politician, and author that loved Estes Park and RMNP. He built himself a cabin (pictured), and a couple more for guests. The William Allen White Cabins are located just south of the Moraine Park Visitor Center and were added to the National Register of Historic Places (NRHP) in 1973, with the distinction of being the first property in RMNP to seek the NRHP designation.

Above right: The Ute Meadow Trail follows a major route used by Arapaho and Ute Indians, making their way between summer and winter hunting grounds on the Great Plains. It is a scenic journey above timberline, guaranteed to deliver awe inspiring views along the way.

Joe Shipler entered the Kawuneeche Valley in 1879, along the Colorado River, starting a mining boom in the North Fork area that would lead to several mining claims and settlements springing up in the region. Not much remains of Shipler's Cabins. Mr. Shipler lived in his cabin until 1914.

Tailings from one of Joe Shipler's silver mines. You will encounter this waste rock pile on your right, prior to reaching the remains of what's left of Shipler's Cabins.

Joseph Fleshut homesteaded this spot in 1902. He lived in the cabin until 1911, before suddenly leaving and abandoning the structure. It is one of the oldest structures still standing in the Kawuneeche Valley. The cabin and land were purchased in 1918 by John Holzwarth, next door land neighbor, so as to expand his own property and guest offerings.

In 1917, John Holzwarth took advantage of the Homestead Act of 1862 to obtain a 160-acre plot of land near RMNP for his family, that would be transformed over time into a premier fishing and recreation destination known as the Holzwarth Trout Lodge (later called the Never Summer Ranch). With the land acquired from Joseph Fleshut in 1918, Mr. Holzwarth expanded his already successful fishing business by adding a lodge in this lush meadow.

The "Mama Cabin" was built in 1917 and is the oldest remaining cabin at the Holzwarth homestead property. Mrs. Sophia Holzwarth would cook many fish themed and German inspired meals for guests in this building, using her Admiral Blue stove. Everest Gay is seen in front of the cabin wearing a jacket made from buffalo.

Another view of the "Mama Cabin." Swing by the Holzwarth Historic Site in RMNP to check out this cabin, and ten-plus additional structures that include an icehouse, taxidermy shop, multiple guest cabins, and a wood shed from 1921. Visitors to the Holzwarth Historic Site can enjoy an interactive experience via the free tours given from mid-June through Labor Day weekend.

The first two homesteads to be claimed in the Kawuneeche Valley were filed by Annie and Kitty Harbinson in 1895. The sisters grazed their cows in this spot for thirty years, providing valuable milk to the town of Grand Lake. The abundance of sage brush (versus grass) in Harbinson Meadow remains a testament to the original use of this land as a food source.

Abner and Alberta Sprague operated a successful resort from this location during the years of 1910-1940. Sprague Lake is a man-made water feature created by Mr. Sprague to enhance the fishing prospects and overall experience of Sprague Lodge guests. The original lodge used to be where the current parking lot is located.

An older cabin sits near the Sprague Lake parking lot, and near where the Sprague Lodge used to be. A bit of trivia: When RMNP instituted a $3 entrance fee in 1939, Mr. Abner Sprague was the first person to pay it.

RMNP is a magical place in the winter. The various landscapes are transformed, with additional recreational opportunities becoming available (winter hiking, snowshoeing, backcountry skiing, winter mountaineering, ice climbing, and more). No matter the season, leaving RMNP is always bittersweet.

14

SEVERANCE, COLORADO
WHERE THE GEESE FLY AND THE BULLS CRY!

Originally intended to be named Tailholt, a clerical error was made when Mr. David E. Severance filed paperwork for the first post office. This mistake resulted in the town name becoming Severance.[1] The Severance Post Office has been in operation since 1894.[2]

The Severance economy in the early-to-late 1900s revolved around sugar beets. The town proved to be an important sugar beet receiving station and dump for the Great Western Sugar Company (GWSC), with the GWSC starting operations in 1905 at their facility in nearby Windsor. The Great Western Railway ceased operations in 1985, taking from Severance its connection to the GWSC, and its biggest cash cow. Or did it?

Today, Severance's biggest claim to fame is its world-famous Rocky Mountain Oysters. Since 1959, Bruce's Bar and Restaurant has been serving the local delicacy to people from all over the nation. The tradition continues today, with many visitors to the area coming specifically to try out Bruce's magnificent Rocky Mountain Oysters.[3]

FASCINATING FACTS FROM THE PAST ABOUT SEVERANCE

1907: Fred Austin, from Fort Collins, was reported to be in the care of his sister living in Severance. His stay being due to a severe case of typhoid fever.[4]

1910: The newspaper thought it was important enough to print that Dave Severance, the son of the founder of Severance, Colorado, would be spending Thanksgiving with his parents that year.[5]

1911: It was announced in *The Delta Independent* that Mr. and Mrs. Dave E. Severance, pioneers of, and the namesake of the town of Severance, were visiting their son in Delta, Colorado.[6]

1922: Hally Heaton Hall, born and raised in Severance, passed away at the young age of twenty-eight, after his third bout of pneumonia. This last time, his illness was described as being "double pneumonia" (both lungs), resulting in death after nine days.[7]

1957: Twenty-six friends attended a farewell supper for David Wyman and his family. Mr. Wyman purchased a Mobile Oil service station and bulk plant, requiring the move to Severance.[8]

Mr. Bruce Ruth opened Bruce's Bar, located in the former Severance Recreation Hall, in 1957. The year 1959 would see the introduction of "cowboy caviar" to the menu. Since then, Bruce's Bar, and the town of Severance, have become notorious for tasty Rocky Mountain Oysters (bull testicles). Visitors come from all over the state and nation to grub on some gonads at Bruce's Bar.

Above left: The various murals on the outside of the Bruce's Bar building were painted in 1972. From a bull being wrangled, to humorous dialogue between bulls, several drawings adorn the external front walls of the establishment.

Above right: The Severance Post Office has been in service since 1894.

In the early years, a horse and buggy were used to transport Severance mail to and from the nearby towns of Eaton and Windsor.

An interesting "airplane hangar" type steel structure located next to the Severance Post Office. Currently, the building is divided into private residences.

Right: Severance Community Church holds its services inside the Old Town Hall. Brownell Park is in front of the building and features a small playground, gazebo, basketball court, and picnic tables.

Below: An older looking building near the Severance Community Church. There are some interesting old vehicles parked next to it.

Lakeview Cemetery was established way back in 1880.

A beautiful sunset closes out the evening at Lakeview Cemetery.

A personal and powerful message inscribed on a headstone.

15

TRI-POINTS, COLORADO
THE MEETING OF "3"

A trifinium, tri-point, or tri-state area, is a spot where three state boundaries meet. There are more than sixty tri-points in the United States, with Colorado being part of five of them.

1. Colorado-Kansas-Nebraska
2. Colorado-Kansas-Oklahoma
3. Colorado-Oklahoma-New Mexico
4. Colorado-Wyoming-Utah
5. Colorado-Wyoming-Nebraska[1]

The two most northerly tri-point areas that include Colorado are the Colorado-Wyoming-Utah (CO-WY-UT) and the Colorado-Wyoming-Nebraska (CO-WY-NE) locations. For this book, I will present the CO-NE-WY trifinium, leaving you to find and experience the CO-WY-UT tri-point for yourself. Located at the intersection of the forty-first parallel of north latitude with the twenty-seventh degree of west longitude (Washington Meridian), U.S. Astronomer and Surveyor Oliver N. Chaffee, mapped out and marked the CO-WY-NE site in 1869.[2]

Finding a tri-point in person can be difficult and may involve legally crossing private property. In some cases, as is the case for the CO-WY-NE spot, a vehicle with decent clearance and good tires (with a spare) is essential for traveling the final distance over farmland to the marker.

This gate off County Road 200 marks the final stretch to reach the CO-NE-WY tri-state marker. Though the rest of the way is on private property, respectful visitors should be able to travel the ¾ mile distance to the official marker.

Depending on the time of year you visit, cattle may be present. Use caution finding your way "straight back" along the fence line to the monument. Follow established tire tracks if possible. A vehicle with clearance and good tires is highly recommend for this section.

The official tri-state marker indicating the intersection of Colorado, Wyoming, and Nebraska. The state of Wyoming is within the fence borders, with Colorado to the left of the fence and Nebraska to the right.

16

US-85 (NORTH), COLORADO
THE CANAM HIGHWAY

United States Highway 85 (US-85) is a tri-national roadway connecting the United States to Canada and Mexico. The 1,477-mile highway originally began construction in 1926 and would take until the 1940s to actually stretch all the way to the borders of Canada (Fortuna, ND) and Mexico (El Paso Texas). US-85 enters Colorado from the south near Starkville and exits the state from the north just past Nunn, Colorado. The length of US-85 in Colorado is approximately 309 miles.[1]

Traveling north along US-85 from Brighton, Colorado, this book will cover five historically significant towns. The locations profiled are Platteville, Eaton, Ault, Pierce, and Nunn.

PLATTEVILLE, COLORADO

Due to its location near a major river and overall favorable land, the Platteville area was home to Native Americans, hunters, traders, and trappers. At one point in the 1830s, four forts operated in the region, creating a mecca for trading. Fort Vasquez (1835), Fort Lupton (1836/1837), Fort Jackson (1837), and Fort St. Vrain (1837) were established and executed trades for several years. All four forts were out of commission by 1845.[2]

Fast forward to 1870 when the Denver and Pacific Railroad reach the region. Platteville is established in 1871, with the town becoming incorporated in 1887. In an effort to meet the needs of railroad workers, travelers, and residents from the area, many businesses opened and operated in those early Platteville years. An ice house, cheese factory, brick factory, cobbler, two newspapers, drug store, blacksmiths, two banks, and two bakeries were among the enterprises one could find back in the day.[2]

Today, fewer than 3,000 people live in Platteville. Ranching and farming continue to be dominant endeavors in the region, as they have been for more than a century. Harvest season is so important to the citizens of Platteville that an annual harvest festival has been held every year since 1910.[3] The first event in 1910 was called "Pickle Day," with the most recent one being called "Harvest Daze."[4]

EATON, COLORADO

Named after Colorado pioneer and irrigation genius, Benjamin Harris Eaton, the town of Eaton was incorporated in 1892.[5] It was clear to Mr. Eaton as early as the 1870s that access to water was critical for the long-term success of farming in the historically dry northern region of the state. As such, he spent decades creating sophisticated canals and ditches, several of which are still used today. A few of the projects Mr. Eaton was responsible for include the Larimer County Canal No. 2 (1873), Eaton Ditch (1878-1879), and the High Line Canal in Denver (1879). He also built Kearns Reservoir in 1890.[6]

AULT (A UNIQUE LITTLE TOWN), COLORADO

Eighty-plus years before Ault would become an official town, the area was frequently visited by trappers, traders, miners, explorers, and even soldiers traveling along the Trapper's Trail. First known to be used in 1820 during Stephen H. Long's expedition to find the origins of the Arkansas, Platte, and Red Rivers, the Trapper's Trail was a north-south route that connected Fort Laramie in Cheyenne, Wyoming, to the Santa Fe Trail at Bent's Old Fort in Southern Colorado.[7]

Jump ahead to the 1870s, and the Ault region has enough settlers and a Union Pacific Railroad line to become a thriving community. Ault would officially become incorporated in 1904, named after Alexander M. Ault. Mr. Ault was an early pioneer in the area having his hands in many realms, including flour, grain buying and distribution, ranching, farming, and the railroad. Over time, Ault would become an important agricultural distribution center, serving the region for more than a century.

From its humble population of around 900 residents in 1908,[8] to the current count of around 1,900 inhabitants,[9] this "Unique Little Town" is still going strong. Transportation of goods and agriculture continue to be a part of Ault's economic backbone, along with Ault being the location for the Highland School District headquarters. Since 1907, Ault has hosted an annual Harvest Festival[8].

PIERCE, COLORADO

The Denver Pacific Railroad reached Pierce on November 8, 1869, but it would take until 1918 for the town to become officially incorporated. Named after General John Pierce, president of the Denver Pacific Railroad (USA division), Pierce became a hub for the transportation of agricultural products. The Pierce Post Office has been in operation since 1903.[10]

Nunn (Watch Nunn Grow!), Colorado

Nunn originated as a train stop along the Denver Pacific Railroad (DPR), just like Pierce, Colorado. The DPR route operated north-south between Cheyenne, Wyoming, and Evans, Colorado. Incorporated in 1908, the town was named after Tom Nunn, in honor of his actions. He is credited with stopping a train that was traveling toward a burning bridge near Pierce, thus preventing a potential disaster.[11] The Nunn Post Office has served its citizens since 1905[12].

Fascinating Facts From the Past About Places Along US-85 (North)

1893: Riders of the 5th annual bicycle race from Denver to Platteville faced a strong headwind the majority of the 25-mile distance. Despite the tough conditions, 162 men finished the event.[13]

1904: Colorado pioneer, governor, legendary ditch builder, and namesake for the town of Eaton, Benjamin Harris Eaton passed away after an unsuccessful battle with complications related to diabetes.[14]

1910: *The Greeley Tribune* reported that "Ault is preparing for one of the best baby shows the state has ever seen and every proud mother of the Ault district is sure of winning at least first prize. The baby show is to be one of the biggest attractions at the carnival held this coming Friday".[15]

1917: If you were trying to rent a house in Nunn, back in 1917, you would have been out of luck. No houses were available or vacant. W. D. and L. D. Orion found that truth out when they moved to Nunn from Longmont. They ended up buying a lot and building a residence.[16]

1918: In a strange incident, four-year-old Ruth McLain swallowed a small spring, causing her to choke. Her parents could not dislodge the item, so they drove to Pierce to get help by a doctor. Due to the rough road along the way, the spring was dislodged. Ruth ended up being just fine.[17]

Looking east down Main Street at a few of the historic buildings that can be found in Platteville.

Looking at two structures on the west side of Main Street.

Though the cornerstone for the church building in the picture was laid in 1929, the Platteville United Methodist Church originally began as the Methodist Society in 1863. Meetings were first in members' homes, and their first official church was built in 1882. That church was demolished to build the current one.

An example of a typical cabin constructed in the late 1800s sits near the Platteville Pioneer Museum. Looking through a window, one will find that it is fully furnished and decorated to replicate that era.

A side view of the exquisite brick building that used to house the original Platteville Town Library. Currently, the Platteville Pioneer Museum uses the space. Wondering what's inside that wooden case in the middle of the picture? It is a 1903 Ford Replica built by Mike Blossom in 1973 while he was in high school. He did an amazing job!

A view of one of the entrances into the former Platteville Town Library, showing the founder's block, year built, and neat architecture. In this case, the Woman's Club established the library in 1932.

The St. Nicholas Catholic Church was built in 1946, to replace the original brick chapel that had been in use since 1889. A life-size St. Nicholas statue can be found above the front entrance. (Platteville)

This is the sign encountered just before entering what appears to be private ranch property. The sign is located at the intersection of County Road 40 and County Road 23. Drive to the end of County Road 40 to reach the Fort St. Vrain historical markers. (Platteville)

Marcellin St. Vrain began his "fort career" by working for his brother Ceran at Bent's Old Fort in 1835. After earning his wings and a solid reputation as a capable fort manager at Bent's Old Fort, Marcellin was put in charge of his brother's newly built Fort St. Vrain in 1837. (Platteville)

The Fort St. Vrain historical marker was placed by the Centennial Chapter of the Daughters of the American Revolution in 1911. Interestingly, Marcellin St. Vrain's daughter, Mary Louis, born in 1846, attended the 1911 Fort St. Vrain dedication along with her daughter and grandson. That makes three generations in attendance! (Platteville)

A. J. Eaton, son of Eaton's founder, Benjamin Eaton, built the first two-story brick house in town. Completed in 1888, the home boasts an impressive stone foundation and original amenities that included a parlor, loft, sitting room, pantry with pastry table, full basement with a fruit cellar, coal storage, and a massive cesspool measuring 8 feet in diameter and 16 feet deep. Currently, the A. J. Eaton house is home to the Eaton Area Historical Society.

Above left: Benjamin Harris Eaton (1833-1904) is the namesake for the town of Eaton, which was incorporated in 1892. Mr. Eaton was the 4th Governor of Colorado, serving from 1885-1887. He was known for his honesty, charity, and vital irrigation systems that still serve the area today.

Above right: The home at 420 Elm Street was built in 1901 by Mr. William L. Petrikin. He is responsible for bringing the Great Western Sugar Company (GWSC) to Eaton, followed by becoming President of the GWSC later in his career. Northern Colorado continues to be a dominant player in the sugar beet industry 120+ years later.

E. G. Steele built this home in 1898. He was a savvy entrepreneur, owning several businesses in Eaton. Mr. Steele was also on the town board and was heavily involved in waterworks related projects.

The Amanda K. Alger Memorial Methodist Episcopal Church was built in 1925 in the Gothic Revival style. Though the name has changed (slightly) to the Alger Memorial Methodist Episcopal Church, the support and service provided to the community for almost 100 years has not changed. In fact, the church was added to the National Register of Historic Places in 2006, with "social significance" being a major contributing factor for the designation. (Eaton)

Above left: Albert Eaton constructed this home in 1896. Mr. Eaton was the mayor of Eaton from 1907-1908.

Above right: Built in 1890, the Eaton Congregational Church was the only house of worship in Eaton until 1900. Governor Benjamin Eaton donated the land and bricks for the church. Rev. John King was the first pastor.

Left: The marker for Dr. John C. Carlson can be found in front of the Eaton Town Hall Building. Erected in 1928, the memorial honors Mr. Carlson's life and selfless service to citizens of Weld County for twenty-five years (1902-1927).

Below: There's no denying that Ault is "A Unique Little Town," and this sign will ensure you know that when entering via US-85.

Above: Built in 1907, this structure originally served as Hotel Joy. Currently, Cinn Sations, home of the Krautburger, and Tangles Salon, occupy the building.

Right: The First Baptist Church of Ault used this building after it was built in 1921. Living Hope Community Church, established in 1953, now occupies the space.

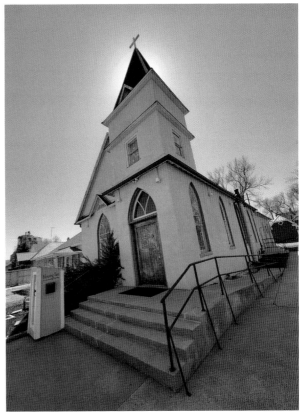

Liberty Park celebrates the hard work and sacrifices made by the founders of Ault, and the men and women that have fought bravely and selflessly through the military to secure our freedom. Replicas of the Statue of Liberty can be found in many towns throughout Colorado, just like in Ault.

Ault High School was designed by architect Sidney G. Frazier and built in 1921. Interestingly, there are two "statements" built into the front of the school. One quote states: "Education is the Process of Fitting Youth for the Responsibilities of Life." The other quote reads: "Every Addition to True Knowledge is an Addition to Human Progress." The building served as the high school until 1976, becoming the Ault Middle School after that until 1992.

Union Pacific (UP) Caboose 2526 was obtained from the defunct Chicago, Rock Island and Pacific Railroad in 1980 (then known as Rock Island Caboose 17203). With the reduction of cabooses being used with trains, UP retired Caboose 2526 in 1985. It was donated to the town of Ault in 1986.

The Pierce town sign, next to the Union Pacific railroad. Also in view is one of the Roggen Farmers' Elevator Association facilities. This site can hold approximately 387,000 bushels of grain.

A beautiful 1936 Cadillac parked on Main Street. (Pierce)

The front of the Pierce Senior Citizens Center is a straight up jigsaw puzzle! The building design, hand painted business name, and color matching awning really caught my eye. Back in the day, the Pierce Post Office was relocated here (1907) from its original location at the Pierce train depot.

The Plains Market & Liquor Store operates out of the bottom floor of this massive brick building, which was built in 1904. The top floor holds three separate residences, consisting of a total of five bedrooms and four bathrooms. The Plains Market & Liquor Store motto is fantastic: "If We Don't Have It, You Don't Need It".

The First Methodist Church was built in 1908. The congregation's name was changed in 1968 to the United Methodist Church.

Bicentennial Park is a grassy area off US-85 that contains a historical marker honoring pioneer residents Mr. & Mrs. L. N. Priddy. Also in view is the Pierce water tower.

The town sign one encounters when entering Nunn from the south via US-85. Watch Nunn Grow! And grow it has, from an estimated population of 143 in 1910, to 416 in 2010.

The Nunn Elevator is part of the much larger Roggen Farmers' Elevator Association, which is a major supplier of grain in Colorado. As of 2019, the Nunn facility has the ability to store 144,000 bushels of grain.

Nunn Motor Company. Unfortunately, information is scarce on this building, its origin, or past history.

The former Nunn Municipal Hall was a constructed during 1933-1934, as part of the Depression-era Works Progress Administration (WPA) program to put Americans to work. Currently, the building is home to the High Plains Historical Society and the Nunn Museum.

Above left: The Nunn Museum contains a plethora of interesting historical artifacts, insider and outside of the building. The Murphy's Blacksmithing building is in view, along with various farming implements.

Above right: The Nunn Centennial marker (1906-2006) is located on the west side of US-85, just north of 3rd Street. It was dedicated on August 19, 2006.

Part of the Denver Pacific Railway historical marker inscription reads, "When the Union Pacific Railroad decided to go through Wyoming instead of through Colorado, many people moved from the territory. Former Governor John Evans rescued Colorado Territory by promoting a connecting railroad from Denver to Cheyenne. Grading began in 1868, and the road was completed in June 1870. The tracks ran through this point. In 1880, the Denver Pacific was absorbed by the Union Pacific." (Nunn)

The Union Pacific railroad tracks run right along the Bellmore Farms property. (Nunn)

Above left: The Mountain View Cemetery arched sign was built by Mr. Fred M. Kovach and friends, as a tribute to his wife, Mrs. Wilma Kovach. (Nunn)

Above right: There are over 600 people buried at Mountain View Cemetery. You will find many examples of the intricate Woodmen of the World (WOW) markers, as well as gravesites that date back to the 1898 Spanish-American War (Nunn).

Imagine my surprise seeing this oil rig escape pod sitting in the field next to the Mountain View Cemetery! The Ocean Saratoga drilling platform was built in 1976 and was retired in 2015. It was a semi-submersible structure capable of operating in water depths of 500-3,000 meters. The Ocean Saratoga could drill down to a maximum depth of 25,000 feet. (Nunn)

Majuro is the capital city for the Marshall Islands and the port of registry for the Ocean Saratoga. The oil rig sailed under the Republic of the Marshall Islands flag. The escape capsule can accommodate up to twenty-eight people, would have radios to summon assistance, and contain a small supply of food and water. How frightening would it be to bob around a furious ocean in this cramped space, waiting to be rescued?! (Nunn)

SITE LOCATIONS

CHAPTER 1 — BELLVUE, COLORADO 80512
Old Jacob Flowers Store & Post Office: 2929 N. County Road 23
Bellvue Store: 5032 Rist Canyon Road
Pleasant Valley Church of Christ: 5220 Rist Canyon Road
Watson Lake SWA & Bellvue-Watson Fish Hatchery: 4936 W. County Road 52E
Noosa Yoghurt Factory + Pleasant Valley School: 4120 N. County Road 25E

CHAPTER 2 — FRANKTOWN, COLORADO 80116
Castlewood Canyon State Park: 2989 CO-83
Franktown Marker: 1867 N. CO-83
Russellville Ranch: 10027 Tomichi Road
Pikes Peak Grange No. 163: 3093 N. CO-83
Franktown Cemetery: 2128 N. CO-83

CHAPTER 3 — GREENLAND, COLORADO 80118
Greenland Ranch: Intersection of E. Greenland Road & E. Noe Road
Abandoned Structures: Along E. Noe Road between Greenland Ranch and Greenland Open Space
Greenland Open Space + Burial: North Trail located at 1532 E. Noe Road
Historic Allis Ranch: 1469 E. Noe Road

CHAPTER 4 — HEREFORD, COLORADO 80732
Hereford Community Church: 67090 Circle Drive
Home of Peace Cemetery: Weld County Road 89 just North of Grover, Colorado (40.886516,-104.219405)
Vacant Structure with Camper: Circle Drive just North of the Hereford Community Church
Vacant Home + Blue Car: Intersection of Weld County Road 390 & Hereford Street
Vacant Garage: Intersection of Weld County Road 390 & Roosevelt Street
"Triangle Top" Abandoned House: Travel South on Weld County Road 79 from Weld County Road 136 (40.9689631,-104.3157609)
Abandoned Homestead with Moon: Intersection of County Road 77 & County Road 126 (40.901464,-104.335459)
Abandoned White Home: Mystery location. You will have to explore the area to find it!

Chapter 5 — Hygiene, Colorado 805303/80533
Church of the Brethren: 7861 Hygiene Road
Hygiene Post Office: 11830 N. 75th Street
The Mountain Fountain: 11809 N. 75th Street
Vacant Country Corner Store: Directly across the street from The Mountain Fountain
United Methodist Church of Hygiene: 7542 Hygiene Road

Chapter 6 — Johnstown, Colorado 80534/80543
Johnson's Corner + Cinnamon Rolls: I-25 at Exit 254 (2842 SE Frontage Road)
Johnson's Corner Chapel: Directly across the street from Johnson's Corner Truck Stop (6501 E. County Road 16)
Masonic Temple: 3 S. Rutherford Avenue
State Farm Building: 118 W. Charlotte Street
Radio Station Building: 2 S. Parish Avenue
Sidewalk Clock: 1 N. Parish Avenue
Parish House Museum: 701 Charlotte Street
St. John the Baptist Catholic Church: 801 Charlotte Street
Country Gospel Cowboy Church: 25 S. Denver Avenue
Johnstown Cemetery: 23101 County Road 13

Chapter 7 — Keota, Colorado 80729
Town Sites: Intersection of Roanoke Avenue and Tioga Avenue
Keota Cemetery: Intersection of County Road 105 & County Road 100 (40.71425, -104.06882)

Chapter 8 — Louisville, Colorado 80027
Louisville Museum + Historic Jordinelli House: 1001 Main Street
Little Brick School: 801 Grant Street
Italian Neighborhood House Example 804 La Farge Avenue
Louisville United Methodist Church: 741 Jefferson Avenue
Historic Romero House: 701 Garfield Street
Louisville Arboretum: Located on Via Appia Way between the Louisville Recreation Center and the Police Department
Louisville Law Enforcement Memorial at Helburg Park: 992 W. Via Appia Way
Historic Lockner Building: 1006 Pine Street
Harper Lake and Wildlife Sanctuary: N. McCaslin Blvd & Washington Avenue (39.978287 -105.164490)
Louisville Cemetery: 2105 Empire Road

Chapter 9 — Louviers, Colorado 80125/80131
Louviers Sign & Flagpole: In the median across from the church at 7595 Louviers Blvd.
Louviers Village Clubhouse: 7885 Louviers Blvd.
Louviers Community Presbyterian Church: 7933 Louviers Blvd.
Trail to Original Du Pont Factory + Railroad Tracks: Park at the tiny lot located at the intersection of Main Street & Louviers Drive.

Chapter 10 — Masonville, Colorado 80538/80541
Masonville Mercantile: 9120 N. County Road 27 (Buckhorn Road)
Replica of Wild West Town & Relics: Across the street from the Masonville Mercantile
Old Building by the Masonville Mercantile: Across the street at 9155 W. County Road 38 E
Buckhorn Presbyterian Church: 8762 N. County Road 27

Chapter 11 – Pawnee National Grassland, Colorado 80729

PNG Auto Bird Tour: From I-25, take CO-14 east ~47 miles to County Road 77. Take a left onto County Road 775 (north), followed by going left (west) onto County Road 96. Bird Tour Kiosk will be on the right, just down the road. (40.683568749117484, -104.35411187791836)

The Pawnee Buttes Trailhead: From I-25, take CO-14 east ~60 miles to County Road 105. Take a left onto County Road 105 (north), followed by going right (east) onto County Road 104. Reach County Road 111 from County Road 104 and go left (north) all the way to the trailhead parking lot (road will loop to the right before parking area). (40.808099871053265, -103.98930693497036)

Chapter 12 – Red Feather Lakes, Colorado 80545

Historic Robinson Cabin: 711 Prairie Divide Road (County Road 67J)

Chimney: Near the intersection of Prairie Divide Road and Nokomis Road

Chapter 13 – Rocky Mountain National Park (RMNP), Colorado 80517

Historic Beaver Meadows Visitor Center: 1000 US-36

Historic Moraine Park Discovery Center: 3 Bear Lake Road (40.358744660804405, -105.58244123541843)

William Allen White's Cabin: Just South of the Moraine Park Discovery Center on Bear Lake Road

Ute Meadow Trail: Trail Ridge Road (40.393515511913265, -105.69535602828252)

Shipley's Silver Mine & Ruins via the Colorado River Trailhead: North of Grand Lake on Trail Ridge Road (40.40126490936013, -105.84878783373553)

Holzwarth's Historic Site: North of Grand Lake on Trail Ridge Road (40.37269954819784, -105.854972159092)

Harbison Meadow: North of Grand Lake on Trail Ridge Road (40.28224139410331, -105.83852593759426)

Historic Sprague Lake & Resort: Sprague Lake Road off Bear Lake Road (40.32041892095952, -105.60818923806873)

Chapter 14 – Severance, Colorado 80546

Bruce's Bar and Restaurant: 123 1st Street

Severance Post Office: 320 1st Street

Interesting Apartment Building: Next to the Post Office

Severance Community Church: 336 1st Street

FinishLine Building: 145 4th Avenue

Lakeview Cemetery: 32815 CO-257, Windsor, CO 80550

Chapter 15 – Tri-points of Colorado

Colorado-Nebraska-Wyoming Tri-point: 41.001665, -104.053178

Chapter 16 – U.S. Highway 85, Colorado (traveling North – Platteville to Nunn)

Platteville, CO 80650:

The Silver Spur & other historic buildings: 613 Main Street (Eastern)

Western side of Main Street: 602 Main Street

Platteville United Methodist Church: 316 Elizabeth Avenue

The Platteville Museum: 502 Marion Avenue

St. Nicholas Catholic Church: 520 Marion Avenue

Fort St. Vrain: Exit U.S. Highway 85 and take CO-60 W to County Road 40. Take County Road 40 west (left) until reaching the end of the road and the marker (40.279151624770556, -104.85467120359793)

EATON, CO 80615:

Eaton Area Historical Society & Museum: 207 Elm Avenue
Benjamin Harris Eaton Statue: Intersection of Collins Street and S. Elm Avenue
W. L. Petrikin House: 420 Elm Avenue
E.G. Steele House: 332 Elm Avenue
Alger Memorial United Methodist Church: 303 Maple Avenue
Albert Eaton House: 328 Maple Avenue
Rocky Mountain View Church: 325 2nd Street
Eaton Town Hall + Dr. John C. Carlson Memorial: 223 1st Street

AULT, CO 80610 :

Ault Town Sign: Entering Ault via U.S. Highway 85 when traveling north into town
Historic Building with Cinn Sations & Tangles Salon: 103 1st Avenue
Living Hope Community Church: 204 A Street
Liberty Park and Statue of Liberty: Intersection of West 1st Street and 1st Avenue
Ault High School: 208 West 1st Street
Train Display: Across the road from 115 U.S. Highway 85

PIERCE, CO 68767:

Railroad Tracks & Town Sign: Intersection of U.S. Highway 85 & E. Main Avenue (40.63551484319814, -104.75187131776795)
36 Caddy and Historic Buildings: Near the intersection of E. Main Street & 2nd Street
Pierce Senior Citizens Center: 221 E. Main Avenue
Plains Market & Liquor Store: 139 E. Main Street
First United Methodist Church: 429 3rd Street
Bicentennial Centennial Park: West side of U.S. Highway 85, just north of Shafer Avenue

NUNN, CO 80648:

Nunn Town Sign: Entering Nunn via U.S. Highway 85 when traveling north into town from Pierce
Nunn Elevator, Inc.: East side of U.S. Highway 85, just north of 5th Street
Nunn Motor Co.: 927 4th Street
Museum of The High Plains Historical Society: 755 3rd Street
Nunn Centennial Marker: West side of U.S. Highway 85, just north of 3rd Street
Denver Pacific Railway Historic Marker: East side of U.S. Highway 85 when leaving Nunn, just south of County Road 100
Bellmore Farms Building & Railroad Tracks: East side of U.S. Highway 85, just north of 5th Street
Mountain View Cemetery: County Rd 29 ½ (40.72781192540124, -104.78290417698928)

ENDNOTES/BIBLIOGRAPHY

INTRODUCTION

1 Time Line of Historic Events. (n.d.). Retrieved October 10, 2021, from https://www.nps.gov/romo/learn/historyculture/time_line_of_historic_events.htm

2 Fort Jackson (Colorado). (2021, May 05). Retrieved October 10, 2021, from https://en.wikipedia.org/wiki/Fort_Jackson_(Colorado)

3 The Homestead Act of 1862. (n.d.). Retrieved October 10, 2021, from https://www.archives.gov/education/lessons/homestead-act

4 Lynch, N. (n.d.). Railroads: A brief history of the railroad in Northern Colorado. Retrieved October 10, 2021, from https://greeleymuseums.com/history-of-the-railroad/

Park statistics. (n.d.). Retrieved October 10, 2021, from https://www.nps.gov/romo/learn/management/statistics.htm

CHAPTER 1: BELLVUE, COLORADO

1 Bellvue, Colorado. (2020, November 30). Retrieved May 26, 2021, from https://en.wikipedia.org/wiki/Bellvue,_Colorado

2 Sladek, R. (2005). *COLORADO STATE REGISTER OF HISTORIC PROPERTIES NOMINATION FORM - Flowers Store* (p. 14) (United States, TATANKA HISTORICAL ASSOCIATES, INC.).

3 Dunn, M., & *, N. (2018, September 06). The flowers of bellvue. Retrieved May 26, 2021, from https://www.northerncoloradohistory.com/flowers-bellvue

4 Cause of Sickness At Fort Collins. (1900, December 21). *North Park Union,* Volume 5, Number 19, p. 4.

5 SOMEBODY KILLED A DEER NEAR BELLVUE. (1915, January 1). *The Weekly Courier*, p. 8.

6 Bellvue has a population of nearly 300. (1903, December 30). *The Weekly Courier*, p. 8.

7 Bellvue demographics. (n.d.). Retrieved February 25, 2021, from https://www.point2homes.com/US/Neighborhood/CO/Bellvue-Demographics.html

8 Three Hundred Feet of Track Go Out at Bellvue; All the Bridges in Rist Canon Are Destroyed. (1918, June 22). *Loveland Daily Herald,* Volume 9, Number 170, p. 1.

9 FISH HATCHERY AT BELLVUE READY FOR HATCHING EGGS. (1925, February 13). *The Estes Park Trail,* Volume IV, Number 45, p. 1.

Chapter 2: Franktown, Colorado

1 Franktown, Colorado. (2021, May 16). Retrieved May 31, 2021, from https://en.wikipedia.org/wiki/Franktown,_Colorado

2 V., P. (2018, August 14). Franktown Cemetery. Retrieved May 31, 2021, from https://www.dar.org/national-society/historic-sites-and-properties/franktown-cemetery

3 FRANK WHEELER PASSES AWAY. (1913, April 25). *The Record Journal of Douglas County*, p. 1.

4 Turkey Club Will Hold Meeting Near Franktown. (1932, October 6). *The Englewood Herald,* Volume XXII, Number 11, p. 1.

5 TWO CASES OF INFANTILE PARALYSIS REPORTED AT FRANKTOWN THIS WEEK. (1939, October 13). *The Record Journal of Douglas County*, p. 1.

6 Franktown, Parker play host to Olympic torch runners on June 23. (1984, June 18). *Douglas County News-Press,* Volume 92, Number 218, p. 6.

7 Franktown will celebrate the 125th anniversary of the town post office. (1987, August 8). *Douglas County News-Press,* Volume 95, Number 263, p. 12.

Chapter 3: Greenland, Colorado

1 Case, L. (2020, August 27). Monumental happenings and Histories: Greenland (Colorado), a beautiful place. Retrieved June 06, 2021, from https://gazette.com/thetribune/monumental-happenings-and-histories-greenland-colorado-a-beautiful-place/article_fd88d886-a7eb-11e9-a8a4-735cf3a8cc45.html

2 Chotzinoff, R. (2016, April 02). Our town. Retrieved June 06, 2021, from https://www.westword.com/news/our-town-5055414

3 POSTOFFICE CHANGES. (1877, December 8). *Colorado Springs Gazette*, p. 2.

4 Freed by Woman's Confession. (1905, September 29). *The Erie News,* Volume 3, Number 18, p. 5.

5 A NARROW ESCAPE. (1913, June 6). *The Elbert County Tribune,* Volume 29, Number 36, p. 1.

6 BUYS PUREBRED MILKING SHORTHORNS. (1952, November 25). *The Adams County News,* Volume 43, Number 48, p. 4.

7 Breeds of LIVESTOCK, Department of animal science. (n.d.). Retrieved March 17, 2021, from http://afs.okstate.edu/breeds/cattle/milkingshorthorn/index.html/

8 1,360-acre parcel in southern DC sells for $1-million-plus. (1980, December 12). *Douglas County News-Press,* Volume 89, Number 43, p. 9.

Chapter 4: Hereford, Colorado

1 Lynch, N. L. (n.d.). Weld County Towns: The First 150 Years - Hereford. Retrieved June 6, 2021, from https://history.weldgov.com/files/sharedassets/history/documents/county-150/weld-county-towns/d9cc7a30aa8922483323.pdf

2 General. (1917, June 14). *The Raymer Enterprise,* Volume 8, Number 5, p. 2.

3 Much Small Pox at Hereford. (1919, November 28). *The Keota News,* Volume 9, Number 29, p. 3.

4 TRIPS PLANNED ACROSS PLAINS TO HEREFORD INN. (1923, July 4). *The Mirror - UNC,* Volume 5, Number 36, p. 1.

5 HEREFORD HOSPITAL FOR CANCER READY IN SHORT TIME. (1923, November 29). *The Raymer Enterprise,* Volume 14, Number 31, p. 1.

6 Society. (1929, January 17). *The Mirror - UNC,* Volume 11, Number 15, p. 2.

Chapter 5: Hygiene, Colorado

1 What's in a Name: HYGIENE, Colorado - Visit Longmont, Colorado. (n.d.). Retrieved June 07, 2021, from https://www.visitlongmont.org/things-to-do/museums-history/longmont-history/hygiene-co/

2 Page 14 Advertisements. (1891, February 5). *Colorado Farmer,* Volume 38, Number 6, p. 14.

3 Hygiene. (1901, April 26). *Longmont Ledger*, p. 2.

4 PICTURESQUE CAREER IS CLOSED WITH DEATH OF RALPH BLACKBURN. (1926, March 6). *The Daily Times,* Volume XXXII, Number 68, p. 1.

5 J. B. SMITH, PIONEER, ILL AT LOCAL HOSPITAL. (1926, March 18). *The Daily Times,* Volume XXXII, Number 78, p. 1.

6 COUNCIL OF RURAL WOMEN TO BE ENTERTAINED NEXT WEEK AT HYGIENE SCHOOL. (1926, May 28). *The Daily Times,* Volume XXXII, Number 139, p. 1.

CHAPTER 6: JOHNSTOWN, COLORADO

1 HARVEY J. Parish & JOHNSTOWN HISTORY. (n.d.). Retrieved June 10, 2021, from https://www.johnstownhistoricalsociety.org/jtown.html

2 Johnstown, Colorado. (2021, March 07). Retrieved June 10, 2021, from https://en.wikipedia.org/wiki/Johnstown,_Colorado

3 Disastrous Storm at Johnstown. (1905, May 24). *The Loveland Register,* Volume XI, Number 21, p. 1.

4 DAIRY DAY IS NOW IN LIST FOR THE YEAR. (1912, February 15). *The Greeley Tribune,* Volume 42, Number 12, p. 8.

5 Postoffice Safe Robbed. (1915, October 15). *Colorado Farm & Ranch (Eads),* p. 6.

6 AUTO TRUCK FREIGHT ROUTE VIA JOHNSTOWN WILL IE ESTABLISHED. (1918, February 18). *Loveland Daily Herald,* Volume 9, Number 66, p. 4.

7 JOHNSTOWN HAS BEST RURAL SCHOOL IN UNITED STATES. (1922, December 29). *The Estes Park Trail*, p. 1.

CHAPTER 7: KEOTA, COLORADO

1 Goodland, J. (n.d.). *Homesteading and Hope: Keota, Colorado, 1888- Present* (pp. 6-10, Publication). doi:https://www.historycolorado.org/sites/default/files/media/document/2018/keota_primary_resource_set.pdf

2 Pawnee National Grassland. (2021, June 28). Retrieved June 29, 2021, from https://en.wikipedia.org/wiki/Pawnee_National_Grassland

3 Jessen, K. (2017, June 10). Clyde Stanley recognized by Michener in 'Centennial'. Retrieved October 10, 2021, from https://www.reporterherald.com/2017/06/10/clyde-stanley-recognized-by-michener-in-centennial/

4 For Grain Experiments. (1911, February 18). The Idaho Springs Siftings-News, Volume 3, Number 42, p. 2.

5 Nine Months School for Keota District. (1913, March 14). The Keota News, Volume 2, Number 43, p. 1.

6 NEWS NOTES OF THE DAY. (1918, January 4). The Keota News, Volume 7, Number 34, p. 1.

7 First Keota Community Fair a Success. (1922, September 8). The Keota News, Volume 12, Number 18, p. 1.

8 Keota Lad Dies Under Peculiar Condition. (1923, February 13). Fort Collins Courier, p. 1.

CHAPTER 8: LOUISVILLE, COLORADO

1 Conarroe, C. (n.d.). History of Louisville. Retrieved June 23, 2021, from https://www.louisvillechamber.com/louisville-history/

2 Louisville, Colorado. (2021, March 16). Retrieved June 24, 2021, from https://en.wikipedia.org/wiki/Louisville,_Colorado

3 NORTHERN COAL STRIKE HAS BEEN SETTLED AT LAST. (1901, May 3). *New Castle Nonpareil,* p. 3.

4 Knight Templar Trip to Louisville. (1901, June 8). *The Florence Daily Tribune,* Volume 7, Number 85, p. 4.

5 LOUISVILLE LOCALS. (1905, August 11). *The Erie News,* Volume 3, Number 11.

6 Louisville & Lafayette Woodmen Celebrate At Eldorado Springs. (1906, August 4). *The News Free Press,* Volume 9, Number 5, p. 1.

7 Louisville Police combat burglary with I.D. program. (1977, June 1). *The Star Courier,* Volume 1, Number 20, p. 4.

Chapter 9: Louviers, Colorado

1 Yongli. (2015, November 10). Louviers. Retrieved June 27, 2021, from https://coloradoencyclopedia.org/article/louviers

2 McManus, C. (2013, December 12). Cleanup at Explosives plant half done. Retrieved June 27, 2021, from https://coloradocommunitymedia.com/stories/cleanup-at-explosives-plant-half-done,108192

3 Louviers, Colorado. (2021, February 07). Retrieved June 27, 2021, from https://en.wikipedia.org/wiki/Louviers,_Colorado

4 Npgallery asset detail. (n.d.). Retrieved June 27, 2021, from https://npgallery.nps.gov/AssetDetail/NRIS/99000710

5 Louviers Du Pont Plant Notes 50th Anniversary. (1958, June 12). *The Douglas County News*, p. 1.

6 NANCY MOORE ONE OF TOP FINALISTS IN MISS AMERICA CONTEST. (1965, September 16). *The Douglas County News*, p. 1.

7 DUPONT TO CEASE DYNAMITE MANUFACTURE THIS SUMMER. (1971, January 14). *The Douglas County News,* Number 15, p. 1.

8 Louviers Dutch Elm Disease Samples "Pos.". (1974, July 18). *The Douglas County News,* Number 42, p. 17.

9 Sheriff's Report - Plane Crashes Near Louviers. (1974, October 24). *The Douglas County News,* Number 4, p. 22.

Chapter 10: Masonville, Colorado

1 Dunn, M. (2017, December 31). The Masons of Masonville. Retrieved June 27, 2021, from https://www.northerncoloradohistory.com/the-masons-of-masonville/

2 Hunt, P. (n.d.). Frontier Town. Retrieved June 27, 2021, from https://wildwood-ranch.us/mpla/index.php/history/frontiertown.html

3 Dye, L. (1990, January 04). Bones of Rare dinosaur discovered in Colorado. Retrieved June 27, 2021, from https://www.latimes.com/archives/la-xpm-1990-01-04-mn-312-story.html

4 MAN SAID HE WANTED TO SPEND CHRISTMAS WITHOUT CROWD ABOUT HIM. (1912, December 27). *The Weekly Courier*, p. 1.

5 STEELE-MASON WEDDING HELD IN DENVER. (1915, July 30). *Loveland Daily Herald,* Number 303, p. 4.

6 FIRST SLACKER SENT FROM COUNTY IS FREE; MENTALLY UNBALANCED. (1917, November 23). *Loveland Daily Herald,* Volume 8, Number 310, p. 1.

7 Slacker. (2021, January 11). Retrieved April 14, 2021, from https://en.wikipedia.org/wiki/Slacker

8 To Vaccinate Pupils At Masonville School. (1922, November 27). *Fort Collins Courier*, p. 1.

9 MASONVILLE MAN SLAYS BIG MOUNTAIN LION. (1927, March 25). *The Estes Park Trail,* Volume VI, Number 51, p. 12.

Chapter 11: Pawnee National Grassland (PNG), Colorado

1 Pawnee National Grassland. (2021, June 28). Retrieved June 29, 2021, from https://en.wikipedia.org/wiki/Pawnee_National_Grassland

2 Arapaho. (n.d.). Retrieved June 29, 2021, from https://www.fs.usda.gov/wps/portal/fsinternet

3 BIRDS AND ANIMALS. (1904, May 18). *Clear Creek Democrat,* Volume 1, Number 2, p. 2.

4 WIFE, 18 YEARS OLD, KILLS HERSELF AFTER QUARREL. (1917, September 26). *Loveland Daily Herald,* Volume 8, Number 261, p. 4.

5 SKELETONS FOUND AT PAWNEE BUTTES. (1925, January 1). *The Raymer Enterprise,* Volume 15, Number 35, p. 1.

6 Big Liquor Plant Serving Sterling Patrons Closed. (1925, July 31). *The Brush Tribune,* Volume 31, p. 1.

7 Gazette Telegraph, Volume 83, Number 28. (1954, May 16). *Gazette Telegraph,* Volume 83, Number 28, p. 116.

Chapter 12: Red Feather Lakes, Colorado

1 Red Feather Historical Society. (n.d.). Retrieved July 13, 2021, from https://redfeatherhistoricalsociety.org/local-histories/red-feather-lakes-history/the-story-of-red-feather/

2 Red Feather LAKES, COLORADO. (2021, July 11). Retrieved July 13, 2021, from https://en.wikipedia.org/wiki/Red_Feather_Lakes,_Colorado

3 Seniors Sneak to Red feather Lakes. (1936, October 28). *The Rocky Mountain Collegian - CSU Fort Collins,* Volume XLVI, Number 8, p. 1.

4 County Postmasters Will Attend Annual Meet In Washington. (1939, October 5). *The Colorado Transcript,* Number 49, p. 1.

5 SALE OF RED FEATHER LAKES FALLS THROUGH. (1942, August 28). *The Estes Park Trail,* Volume XXII, Number 20, p. 8.

6 All Fish Killed In Three Lakes. (1948, September 9). *The Steamboat Pilot*, p. 10.

7 Cut your own holiday tree at $5 each. (1982, December 8). *The Louisville Times*, p. 44.

8 Arapaho and Roosevelt national FORESTS Christmas Tree permit in Colorado. (n.d.). Retrieved May 05, 2021, from https://www.recreation.gov/tree-permits/225c1015-e631-11ea-8a7e-f638cd389a69

Chapter 13: Rocky Mountain National Park (RMNP), Colorado

1 Time Line of Historic Events. (n.d.). Retrieved October 10, 2021, from https://www.nps.gov/romo/learn/historyculture/time_line_of_historic_events.htm

2 Visitor information: Rocky mountain national park: Grand County, Colorado. (n.d.). Retrieved October 10, 2021, from https://www.visitgrandcounty.com/rmnp/visitor-info

3 7 Things You Didn't Know About Rocky Mountain National Park. (2021, September 29). Retrieved October 10, 2021, from https://www.doi.gov/blog/7-things-you-didnt-know-about-rocky-mountain-national-park

Chapter 14: Severance, Colorado

1 History of the town of severance. (n.d.). Retrieved July 14, 2021, from https://www.townofseverance.org/home/faq/history-town-severance

2 Severance, Colorado. (2020, August 31). Retrieved July 14, 2021, from https://en.wikipedia.org/wiki/Severance,_Colorado

3 Our Story. (n.d.). Retrieved July 14, 2021, from https://brucesbar123.com/our-story

4 UNKNOWN. (1907, October 2). *Fort Collins Courier*, p. 13.

5 LOCAL AND PERSONAL. (1910, November 25). *The Delta Independent,* Volume 28, Number 42, p. 5.

6 Delta County Gets Two Officers in State Auctioneers Association. (1911, September 8). *The Delta Independent,* Volume 29, Number 29, p. 1.

7 HALLY HEATON HALL. (1922, October 28). *The Denver Clarion - University of Denver, Volume 27, Number 6*, p. 4.

8 LOCALS. (1957, August 1). *The Steamboat Pilot*, p. 5.

Chapter 15: Tri-Points, Colorado

1 Tri-state area. (2021, June 15). Retrieved June 27, 2021, from https://en.wikipedia.org/wiki/Tri_state_area

2 Highpointers Club: TRIPOINT COLORADO-NEBRASKA-WYOMING. (n.d.). Retrieved June 27, 2021, from https://highpointers.org/wp-content/uploads/tripoints/pages/3ptCO-NE-WY.html

Chapter 16: US-85 (North), Colorado

1 Elbert, C., Hamilton, A., Macdonald, J., Sanderson, D., Summa, M., & Taylor, S. (2000). End of US Highway 85. Retrieved September 30, 2021, from https://www.usends.com/85.html

2 History: Platteville, CO. (n.d.). Retrieved September 30, 2021, from https://www.plattevillegov.org/2192/History

3 Platteville, Colorado. (2021, September 07). Retrieved September 30, 2021, from https://en.wikipedia.org/wiki/Platteville,_Colorado

4 Harvest daze: Platteville, CO. (n.d.). Retrieved September 30, 2021, from https://www.plattevillegov.org/2301/Harvest-Daze

5 Eaton, Colorado. (2021, September 10). Retrieved October 09, 2021, from https://en.wikipedia.org/wiki/Eaton,_Colorado

6 Fasse, C. (2015, February 21). Windsor's Eaton House earns historic designation. Retrieved October 09, 2021, from https://www.coloradoan.com/story/news/local/windsor/2015/02/21/windsors-eaton-house-earns-historic-designation/23786939/

7 History of Ault. (n.d.). Retrieved October 09, 2021, from https://townofault.org/history-of-ault/

8 Gieck, M. (2006). *Colorado State Register of Historic Properties Nomination Form* (pp. 7-8, Rep.). doi:https://www.historycolorado.org/sites/default/files/media/documents/2018/5wl5026.pdf

9 Ault, Colorado. (2021, September 10). Retrieved October 09, 2021, from https://en.wikipedia.org/wiki/Ault,_Colorado

10 Town of Pierce History. (n.d.). Retrieved October 09, 2021, from https://townofpierce.org/history

11 Warburton, J. (n.d.). Nunn. Retrieved October 09, 2021, from https://www.ghosttowns.com/states/co/nunn.html

12 Nunn, Colorado. (2021, September 07). Retrieved October 09, 2021, from https://en.wikipedia.org/wiki/Nunn,_Colorado

13 BICYCLE CONTEST AT DENVER A TWENTY-FIVE MILE RACE. (1893, June 9). *The Fulford Signal*, p. 2.

14 GOV. EATON DEAD GRAND OLD PIONEER GONE. (1904, November 4). *The Erie News,* Volume 2, Number 22, p. 2.

15 BABY SHOW AT AULT WILL BE A FEATURE. (1910, September 22). *The Greeley Tribune,* Volume 40, Number 44, p. 6.

16 Every Nunn House is Occupied. (1917, January 1). *Routt County Republican*, p. 6.

17 4-YEAR OLD GIRL SWALLOWS SPRING. (1918, January 7). *Loveland Daily Herald,* Volume 9, Number 36, p. 4.